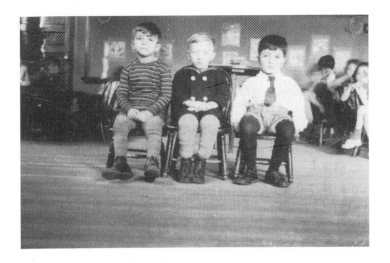

Joseph N. Manfredo (left front) in
kindergarten of Brandegee Grade School in
Utica, New York, circa 1937

ONLY THE LIVING

A Personal Memoir of My Family History

By

JOSEPH N. MANFREDO

Order this book online at www.trafford.com
or email orders@trafford.com

Most Trafford titles are also available at major online book retailers.

Printed in Victoria, BC, Canada.

ISBN: 978-1-4269-2139-1 (sc)

Library of Congress Control Number: 2009941128

*Our mission is to efficiently provide the world's finest, most comprehensive book publishing
service, enabling every author to experience success. To find out how to publish your
book, your way, and have it available worldwide, visit us online at www.trafford.com*

Trafford rev. 11/24/2009

www.trafford.com

North America & international
toll-free: 1 888 232 4444 (USA & Canada)
phone: 250 383 6864 ♦ fax: 812 355 4082

To my parents and the many unsung immigrants who, like them, enriched America with their strong family values, integrity, work ethic, proud culture and a romantic philosophy of life.

EPIGRAPH

I have often, over the years, used my Dad as a sounding board for my frustrations in life. Sometimes my complaints were very serious problems, often as not they were minor. Always I sought that comforting experience of having someone, who loves you unconditionally, listen and understand and be sympathetic. One day, while reciting to him several troubles in my life he placed everything in quiet perspective by observing, "Well, Joey, these are things that only afflict the living." I felt better immediately, recognizing that my problems were the normal, routine bumps in the road of life that one stops feeling only when the journey has ended.

PREFACE

This work was undertaken to assure that at least some of our family legacy should survive the loss of our progenitors. Most of what follows is from personal experience, research of old family documents and recollection of stories told to me by many relatives over many years.

I apologize for any errors of fact or omission you may find and trust you will attribute them to an ageing memory rather than a fertile imagination.

CONTENTS

Illustrations

SALT SCRUB

She cradled the infants' head gently in her left hand to keep it out of the shallow pan of warm water. He gurgled happily, staring up at his mother. With her other hand she softly swished a washcloth through the water and over his torso, arms and legs. She lifted the wooden lid of the small salt cellar that she had brought over from its nail behind the stove. She scooped up small amounts of salt and tenderly sprinkled some over the child's silky flesh. With tears streaming down her cheeks she began to scrub the salt over the babies flesh, slowly at first, then with more deliberate strokes until she had scrubbed his torso, arms and legs several times. She saw no change except for a pinkish hue beginning to emerge. She repeated the procedure again and then again, each time rinsing the child and looking for the change she hoped to see. The skin slowly turned more and more pink. The child whimpered at first, then cried. No matter how hard she tried she could not achieve what she had hoped for. Lifting the baby from the water she wrapped it in a large, soft towel and held it close to her breast. She wept while she comforted it. She was torn with sorrow that she had failed to lighten its olive toned Italian skin and felt deep remorse that she had made the baby cry.

Earlier this morning she had bundled it, placed it in the

carriage and carried it down three flights of stairs to the sidewalk below. She had given birth to it, with the aid of a midwife, in that third floor apartment a few weeks earlier. This was the infant's first trip outdoors and Anna was excited to show it off to the neighbors.

The first to come by was old man Jacobson, the landlord and owner of the building and the clothing store called Jacobson and Marsh located on the first floor. The old man oohed and aahed over the child, remarking how beautiful it was. Then he reached into his vest pocket and withdrew a two and a half dollar gold coin which he placed in Anna's hand. "Save this for the boy," he said. He unlocked the door to the store and disappeared inside.

A few moments later the owner of the shoe store next door, George Flemma, arrived to open shop. He came over to admire the baby and congratulate Anna. He smiled down at the child, tickled his cheek and said, "He has a nice dark complexion, doesn't he." Then, after more compliments and small talk he turned, unlocked his shop and went inside. Anna, focused on that comment, quickly scooped up the carriage and child. She stomped up the stairs, placed the carriage in the kitchen, sat in a chair and anguished over the very Italian complexion of her little one. Then she remembered seeing her mother prepare chickens for roasting by scrubbing them with salt. She recalled that the chicken meat would lighten in color after a brief scrubbing. It was worth a try, she thought.

Years later she would recount this story to me as a humorous, but true, tale of a young woman's tender sensitivity and naïve vanity. She would say how badly she felt, "to this day," about scrubbing me so hard with salt over an innocent comment from a well meaning friend.

My oldest brother, Albert, was born in 1923. It was Mom who chose his name. Years earlier, in Italy, her oldest sister, Nancy, was very much in love with a young Italian boy named Albert. He had joined the Italian army and was ordered to ship out unexpectedly. He was gone from Rome before she had a chance to say goodbye.

Then she learned that hundreds of young recruits were stationed in tents outside Rome awaiting a train to take them to France and the battle lines. She had no transportation so she walked all day until she found the encampment. She wandered anxiously through the camp asking for him. After a time, by sheer luck, she found him. They spent the whole night together talking, holding hands and trying to be brave, surrounded by a thousand other young men who were little more than boys. In the morning he had to leave to board the train. Nancy started her walk back to Rome arriving, exhausted, that evening.

Albert was killed in France. Anna named her first born son Albert, in honor of her sisters' first true love.

Anna gave birth to two more boys, Augustine and Nicholas Jr. Both died of childhood diseases, Augustine at the age of 13 months, Nicholas Jr. two weeks after birth. Mom took those deaths pretty hard. It was months before she could bring herself to launder and put away their last soiled diapers. Dad swore they would no longer, in his words, "make children to fertilize the graveyard." There was no plan to have me.

Then they met the Reverend Vincent Gottuso, a part-time Pentecostal minister and full time furniture re-finisher, who introduced them to the Christian Apostolic Church, a fundamentalist church. Services were conducted in the converted attic of Orazio and Rose Mancuso's hardware store. The Reverend was a former Mafia enforcer, a "leg breaker," before his conversion from Catholicism. The Gottuso family already had six children and their family was still growing. They would eventually have ten. Over time the Reverend convinced Mom and Dad that their practice of birth control was a defiance of the will of God and the child they were preventing might well be one for whom God had planned a great purpose. They converted from Catholicism, conceived me, and spent the rest of their lives waiting for me to fulfill God's grand plan. They never stopped waiting, I suppose.

Mom, whose maiden name was Anna Giangolini, was born

in Vignanello, a small village about 60 kilometers north of Rome, Italy. Her parents, Augusto and Maria Lampredi Giangolini, together with her older brothers and sisters, Joseph, Aneble, Nancy, and Rose moved to Rome when she was still a baby. They lived on a small street just outside the walls of the Vatican, on the right hand side of St. Peter's Cathedral as you face the entrance. It bordered the Sistine Chapel. Many years later, on a vacation trip to Italy, I searched for that street only to find that Vatican City had expanded its' territory and the street on which she lived and played as a child is now behind the walls. There are windows, which you will pass during a tour of the Sistine Chapel, which look down on that street. I did that. No children play there now.

Anna's family was poor and struggling. Her closest childhood friend was the daughter of a very wealthy Roman family. They developed a great affection for Anna and she benefited from their love and generosity. When she was sixteen years of age Anna's family prepared to immigrate to America. Her benefactors asked Anna's parents if they would permit her to stay and be adopted by them. They, of course, refused. On embarkation day Anna was nowhere to be found. Her oldest sister, Nancy, knew where to look and found her hiding with the wealthy family. Anna refused to leave until Aunt Nancy administered a few well placed whacks and forcefully took her away. They left that day for Ellis Island.

Their oldest brother, Joseph Giangolini, had gone on before and lived in Utica, New York. He would sponsor and house them. A younger brother, Aneble, a career Cavalry Officer, remained behind in Italy.

Dad, Nicholas Manfredo, was born in a small country village called Andali, in the province of Catanzaro, state of Calabria. Calabria is in the south of Italy. Part of Calabria appears to be a boot or foot kicking the island of Sicily. That boot has a small heel behind the toe. Andali sits in the tip of the heel, about 6 kilometers north of Cropan. As a child he would stand in the hilltop cemetery behind the village church and stare at the Ionian Sea, 10 kilometers away. He liked to say that he lived his childhood as the archetypical "barefoot boy." No shoes, ragged clothing and hunger ever present. His uncles owned farm land and livestock and were relatively prosperous but devoid of charity. Some family members worked for the Uncles.

Nick's father, Joseph, my Grandfather, had immigrated to America when Nick was still a baby. When Nick was 12 years old his father sent for him and his older brother, Bob, and they left for Ellis Island. His Mother followed a few years later, but that's another story.

Nick and Anna met in Utica, New York, when they "stood up" together (i.e. Maid of Honor and Best Man) at the wedding of Anna's sister Nancy. That, too, is another story.

ANDALI

In 1899, at the turn of the century, Andali, Italy was a small agricultural village in the Province of Catanzaro, nestled in the rolling foothills that rise from the coastal lowlands which stretch to the beaches of the Ionian Sea, ten kilometers to the South. The climate is temperate favoring an agricultural economy. Only a few hundred families lived in this quaint but poor valley. Many maintained small gardens yielding barely enough produce for their own consumption. Some raised a few chickens or other small livestock. Some worked for the prosperous few who owned the larger farms which covered the surrounding rolling hills and vales. Many stood in food lines whenever government food shipments came in to Andali. This was infrequent and limited. A cobblestone road led through the center of the village then rose up and over a small hilltop ridge where it became a narrow dirt road that disappeared down the southern facing slope toward the sea.

Joseph and Teresa Elia Manfredo lived here in a one room stone house with a fireplace and no running water. I know it had a stone fireplace for heating and cooking because Dad, Nicholas, used to tell of the time, as a bare bottomed baby, he fell backward and sat in the fire and burned his bottom. An outhouse sat outside at some distance from the home. A patch of unfenced yard was crammed with tomato plants and a variety of vegetables. Chickens roamed freely pecking at whatever they could find. A wash basin sat on a wooden stand a few feet from the front door. Water was carried from a small creek that wandered nearby or from the community well in the center of the village.

Grandma Teresa was a pretty girl with delicate features but the wiry strength that comes from living an agrarian life style. She and Grandpa Joseph played as children and no one was surprised when the families arranged their marriage. They were both in their teens. His striking good looks and strong will suited Teresa's gentle, quiet and diffident demeanor. Their first child, Robert, was born in 1899. Their second, Nicholas, was born on August 19 of 1900.

Grandpa Joseph was a strict disciplinarian who believed the man of the house was absolute ruler. He expected his wife to bear him children and tend to household chores, help in the garden and otherwise meet his needs. Children should be seen and not heard until they were old enough to work at which time they should do so and contribute to the family well being. Joseph sometimes worked in the fields of the farms owned by his brothers to supplement what he was able to grow in his own yard. He practiced the not uncommon double standard of expecting his woman to be faithful and obedient whereas his own actions were not restricted by such constraints. Hence, when one of the nubile young ladies of the village placed temptation before him he did not feel the need to resist.

One morning, like many others, Joseph stood before the outdoor wash basin, shirtless, suspenders hanging down, face lathered, straight razor in his hand, shaving by the reflection of his face in a small piece of mirror hanging on the wash stand's back board. In that mirror he saw the image of three men rapidly approaching from behind, men he recognized as the father and two brothers of that village girl. They carried ax handles and were clearly bent on avenging the injured honor of the family. As they reached within striking distance Joseph spun around, razor extended, slashing open one face on the first swing, opening a stomach on the return swing. He chased the third man into the wooded hills behind the home. Joseph remained hidden in the hills until he was certain the provincial authorities had left the village after a brief investigation. He made plans to leave for Naples, then for the United States promising Teresa he would send for her when he could. That was how Grandpa Joseph, immigrated to the United States leaving behind a young wife and two baby boys.

To this day Andali, Italy, remains a small town of less than one thousand people. Circling the outskirts of the town is highway SP 259, also known as the John F. Kennedy autostrada.

CHILDHOOD

Little Nicholas would grow up a barefoot boy in impoverished living conditions and innocent of worldly experiences. He was a virgin until his marriage many years later in another country. He liked to joke that his first and only premarital sexual experience occurred when he was around four years old. He and a little girl playmate had noted the peculiar behavior of animals they saw in the fields every day. Chickens, dogs, cats, cattle, sheep, pigs, donkeys....all performed this ritual with apparent enthusiasm. One day they stood in the field watching two donkeys and wondered aloud what it was all about. They discussed it and decided they should try it. Assuming the positions as well as they could recall it they imitated the motion. Of course nothing happened. The concept, as well as the physical ability, was beyond them. They decided the animals were pretty dumb to think this was fun.

Without a husband to provide for them Teresa worked, when she could, in the Uncles fields to put food on the table. They often stood in food lines only to be told it was all gone by the time they reached the head of the line. The boys, Nick and Bob, were cared for much of the time by their Aunt Mary, Teresa's sister.

When Nick reached six years of age his Mother packed a lunch and sent him off to the one room schoolhouse where he sat with his brother, Bob, and a dozen or so boys and girls of various ages. The teacher was a tall, thin man with a dark countenance, a black, bar handle moustache and a permanent scowl. He wore a long sleeved shirt with elastic bands above the elbows and black, pin striped trousers held high by wide, dark suspenders. High top shoes with thick soles added to his imperial stature. He ruled with a loud voice and emphasized his authority by brandishing the wooden spindle from the back of a broken chair. This was his kingdom and his authority was undisputedly supported by the parents of the children.

At the end of each day, when the teacher dismissed the classroom, Nick sat and watched the older children run out. The bigger boys leapt from the stoop and yelled at the top of their lungs expressing their joy at being liberated for the day. The teacher didn't seem to mind and it looked like they were having fun. He thought this was a neat thing to do and admired the big boys. He wanted desperately to belong by imitation but was too shy to dare. This went on for about a month.

Finally, he could resist no longer. At the end of that day, when the school teacher dismissed the class, Nick waited impatiently for the last boy to leap, yelling, off the back stoop. He waited a moment longer then, screwing up his courage, he ran the length of the room and let out a horrendous, joyful war whoop as he leapt clear of the steps. Nick had an unusually powerful set of lungs, even then, and his bellow scared the pasta out of the teacher who leapt to his feet brandishing the wooden spindle, and ran after little Nick. Terrified by the teacher's reaction Nick retreated and stood some distance from the furious man. The teacher ordered him to come back, "Manfredo, vieni qua!" "NO!" Nick declined. Twice. The teacher said, dismissively, "Domani ti prendo." I will get you tomorrow. "Stai fresco," Nick thought, an expression that literally meant "you will stay fresh" but indicated that the teacher would wait a long time for tomorrow. For Nick there never was a tomorrow. His very first month in school, he determined, would be his last.

Each morning he took his lunch, freshly and lovingly made and wrapped by his adoring mother and aunt, walked down the path with his little friends but stopped a few hundred yards before reaching the school. He said goodbye to his friends and watched as they continued down the road to the school house. Nick spent the day playing in the countryside. He wandered the hills, picked wild berries, played with the animals. At the end of the school day he returned and waited by the side of the path for his brother Bob and his friends. Together they walked home arriving in a group as they had left.

One month later the teacher showed up at the house and spoke with his Mom. After the teacher left she told Nick he must return to school or go to work on the Uncle's farm. He was only six years old. He chose to work. He never set foot inside an Italian schoolroom again. He liked to say that at the age of six he enrolled in the school of hard knocks.

The first season he tended sheep and goats. He was paid one penny a day plus one meal a day, at noon. Each day was like the one before. Up before dawn he tended the flocks, coming in at noon to eat lunch with the other men, then went back to the hillsides with the flocks until sunset when the flocks were enclosed for the night. The men were fed on long, wooden tables with several communal sized bowls full of pasta of some sort. There was never any meat. The men ate hungrily and quickly. Little Nick never got enough to eat before the bowls were empty. Consequently he sought food in other ways. Once out of sight, he would crawl underneath the most endowed Nanny goat and milked her directly into his mouth. He subsisted on goat milk and what fruits and raw vegetables he could glean from the crops when no one else was around to watch.

During that first summer season he helped the shepherd move the sheep to higher elevations where grazing pastureland was more plentiful. The shepherd carried a shotgun to ward off wolves.

They slept in a straw hut. Just before retiring the shepherd fired the shotgun twice toward the sky to frighten the wolves away one last time. They took turns on guard duty throughout the night. This young boy sat many frightening nights by the dying fire staring sleepily into the darkness, watching for the glowing eyes of wolves.

One day in September he and a boyfriend were herding the uncle's pigs up into the hills looking for forage. As they topped a ridge they emerged into the uncle's wheat field which had been harvested and stood in hundreds of bound wheat shocks. The ground between shocks was littered with bits and pieces of grain seed, chaff and cuttings. Here there was plenty of forage for the pigs. Down in the small dale at the foot of the hill stood one of the uncle's fig orchards. The limbs were heavy with ripe figs. Nick suggested that his friend go down and steal some figs for them while he remained with the pigs and served as a lookout. Nick promised to whistle a warning if he spotted someone coming. His friend trotted down the hillside and disappeared among the fig trees.

Nick shuffled his feet restlessly, occasionally moved the pigs, and looked down the dirt paths and across the hills for signs of anyone approaching. Time seemed to drag. Flies buzzed in the brilliant sunlight. He shoved his hands into his pockets as he scuffed at the wheat chaff with one toe. He felt a wooden stove match in his pocket.

September, in southern Italy, is hot and sunny, much like Southern California in late summer. But to Nick's young mind that match suggested that a small fire might feel really good. Besides, it was something to do until his friend returned with sweet figs. He swiped together a small circle of wheat clippings and chaff, made a little pile, scratched the match to life on his pants, and lit the pile. He warmed his hands at the fire for several minutes, sweat pouring out from under his little wool cap, when he noticed a few tiny licks of flame begin to travel out of the circle. He stomped with his bare feet, and then thrashed with his wool cap, to no avail. He flailed and stomped furiously which only seemed to encourage the flames to spread. A slight breeze picked up the flames and in seconds the first large wheat shock burst into flame. He decided to run, first chasing the pigs down the path which led back toward the farm, then turned and ran for all he was worth into the hills.

Altogether 600 lire of wheat went up in flames and part of the fig orchard. In 1906 in southern Italy that was a sizable annual income for a wheat farmer.

The smoke soon became visible for miles and his cousins came running to the fire. Every few steps a cousin would pop out of the trees and tell him the uncles were ahead waiting for him. He would turn and run in a different direction only to be intercepted with the same dire warning once again. After tormenting him in this way until they were bored they tied a rope around his ankles and hung him upside down from a stout tree limb. They said they would return soon with the uncles and ran off toward the farmhouse.

As soon as they were out of sight Nick doubled upward, untied his feet, dropped to the ground and ran into the hills. He had, indeed been hung and lived to tell about it. A day or two later he sneaked home where he received a few cuffs and many threats from the uncles.

The uncles wrote to his father, Joseph, in the United States telling him that his little son had burned the year's wheat crop and threatening that if he did not sent 600 lire to pay for it the uncles would put Nick in jail. Joseph, ever affectionate, wrote back "You have him. Lock him up." The debt was never paid.

Little Nicky did not go to jail. The uncles ordered him to work with the men from that time on, hoeing the soil, planting and harvesting crops. It was heavy labor. He was just eight years old.

Nick continued to work for the uncles until he left for America four years later.

But he never felt the need for a hot bonfire in September in southern Italy again.

BEAN POLES AND CHICK PEAS

One day, when Nick was about seven years old, he walked, as he sometimes did, up the cobblestone street to the crest of the hill that overlooked the coastal view. On the way he picked up a long pole lying by the side of a field of string beans, one that had probably been used to tie the bean vines upright. He used the bean pole as a walking stick as he reached the crest of the hill. He stopped in the cemetery behind the church and looked at the gradual descent of small hills and the far off beaches of the Ionian Sea. He imagined the armies of Garibaldi and the invading French swarming the hills and beaches that lay before him all those many years ago. The horizon stretched away forever and he wondered about the outside world that lay beyond his vision. What was out there? What were the people like? He had heard stories of distant cities and countries, especially about America. He tried to imagine how it must be.

After a time he started back over the crest. The descent to the village was steep and it was getting late. He broke into a run pushing the pole over the cobblestones before him. The pole slid and bounced on the cobblestones until, suddenly, it lodged in a crevice between the stones, jamming itself into the pit of his stomach, knocking the wind out of him and rendering him unconscious. He did not recall exactly how it happened.

He remembered awaking, lying on his back and staring up at a circle of the young ladies of the village. They stooped over him, mopping his forehead with wet towels and fussing over him like mother hens. This was more attention than Nick had ever received from girls in his young life and he recalled it with great pleasure. For just a few minutes, he was a village celebrity.

One evening, some seventy-five years later, as he sat at my dinner table in Los Angeles, California, he excused himself before he had finished eating, saying he just didn't feel very well. We were concerned and learned he had not been feeling well for several days, a general malaise, tired, weak.

I drove him to the emergency room at our local hospital. They took a Magnetic Resonance Image which revealed an aneurism, a weak spot in his aorta. It was leaking blood internally with each heart beat. The doctors said surgery to mend this was much too strenuous for a man his age and they preferred to treat it with medications and rest. We agreed. They warned that the weakened wall could rupture at any moment resulting in sudden death. The doctor asked me, if this happened would we want them to attempt "heroics," that is, should they open him up and try to mend it. The doctor recommended against it.

I sat privately with Dad and we discussed it. He asked my opinion. I said if it were me I would not want them to attempt such a drastic procedure. He smiled and told me that he would put his faith in God, that he had lived a good, full life and if it was in God's plan to take him home, well, he was ready. Over the next month he grew steadily stronger, the damage healed and, according to his doctors, the scar tissue made that section of the aorta wall stronger than the rest.

The morning I picked him up from the hospital his Doctors expressed amazement at his rapid recovery. They speculated that this injury may have occurred years ago and remained latent for many years.

Dad's eyes lit up and he said, "You know, when I woke up this morning there were pretty nurses looking down at me and fussing over me and it reminded me of that day in Andali when I was a child and I rammed that same spot with a bean pole and it knocked me out and I woke up surrounded by pretty women fussing over me."

Now, it may or may not have been the cause of his aneurism, but it made such a good story we both accepted it as the truth and told it many times with conviction.

What you are about to read may seem unrelated to this epistle, but it is a necessary piece of colorful Italian historical background leading to one of Dad's favorite childhood expressions involving garbanzo beans, also known as chickpeas.

Giuseppe Garibaldi, who is credited for the eventual unification of Italy, waged much of his later military campaigns against the occupying French forces throughout Sicily and Calabria. Garibaldi's 1862 campaign through Calabria and Sicily sprinkled that area with many rich folk stories which spread even to such tiny hamlets as Andali. And little Nick knew them all and recounted them in later years. The one he particularly liked to tell came up one evening at our dinner table when garbanzo beans were being passed around. He said "I ceci hanno ucciso I Francesi." We asked him to explain what this meant and he did.

It seems that as the French army retreated some of their troops were cut off in many locations throughout Sicily and Italy. When captured they were executed. Some, though, had learned to speak Italian and tried to pass themselves off as Italians. If any doubt remained during questioning of the suspects they were presented with a plate of chickpeas and asked, "What are these?" They answered with the Italian word "Ceci," which was correct. However, the Italian pronunciation crisply places the accent on the first syllable whereas the French pronunciation placed the accent on the second syllable with a decidedly different lilt to the sound. They were executed on the spot.

Hence was born the saying which Nick and his little buddies gleefully repeated, "I ceci hanno ucciso i Francesi."

Or, in English, "Chickpeas killed the French."

Journey To America

The Principe De Piemonte, built in 1889, 430 feet long, 52 feet wide, carried 1,960 passengers that November of 1912. She had departed from Naples, Italy bound for New York City crossing the Atlantic at a steady 14 knots, her twin triple expansion steam engines and twin screws driving her doggedly through rough seas. Seasickness was common. Nights were cold and damp. Accommodations below decks were crowded and suffocating. Some slept on the deck, under the occasional stars, preferring a breath of fresh air. Just four years and two months later she would be sunk by a German submarine off the Irish coast during the hostilities of World War I. But, for now, she traveled safely threatened only by the fierce winter weather of the Atlantic Ocean.

The crew handed out meals which consisted mostly of baloney sandwiches, a, tasteless meat unfamiliar to these spice loving Italians. It was bland to their palates and hard to swallow. During one of Nick's exploratory wanderings into the bowels of the ship he discovered a hold full of onions. These he knew and understood. He, and his brother, Bob, threw the baloney overboard for the fish and replaced it with onions. Eventually some of the other passengers imitated them. For the remainder of the transatlantic voyage they subsisted on onion sandwiches and were, no doubt, followed by schools of fattening fish.

Nick was 12 and his brother Bob 13 years of age. Their father had sent for them. They would soon be old enough to work and take care of themselves. He sent a letter to Teresa, with just enough money for two tickets to America. She, understandably, wanted to emigrate with her children and reunite with her husband but believed he simply did not have the money for her ticket. She knew it was important to remove the boys from the poverty of southern Italy. There seemed no hope of a better future for them if they remained. America was the land of promise. So she made arrangements to take them to Naples for departure. The trip from Andali to Naples, a few hundred miles, must have been difficult. In 1912 the public transportation system in southern Italy was rudimentary. The cobblestone road leaving Andali rose southward over the hills, turned to dirt, then curved a few miles outside the valley, sweeping first northwest then north up the coast to Naples. Somehow they arranged transportation over that early route and reached Naples. The boys embarked for that land across the Atlantic Ocean where it was reputed that the streets were paved with gold. Teresa hugged them one last time and promised she would follow as soon as she could raise the equivalent of thirty American dollars.

Excitement ran high as they pulled into New York Harbor on November 30, 1912. They gaped at the New York skyline and the Statue of Liberty perched on Ellis Island. In long lines they disembarked and filed through the reception procedure which included a physical exam of sorts and filling out forms, often working through translators. Once the process was completed they waited in holding areas for their father, Joseph. He was to be their sponsor. Without someone to claim them and swear to be responsible for their welfare, no immigrant was allowed to leave Ellis Island. Nick and Robert waited.

Joseph eventually arrived, signed off documents for the boys and took them home where they were surprised to learn that they had acquired a stepmother and a half brother. Joseph had taken a common-law wife who bore him a son, Frank.

They first lived in Hamburg, New York, near the railroad tracks for one year. United States law required that children attend school until they were 16 years old. One of Nick and Bob's earliest jobs, when they weren't in school, was to wander the train tracks gathering coal that had fallen off freight trains. What wasn't used to heat their home was sold. In addition the boys took whatever jobs they could find, mostly pick and shovel work. Times were hard. The streets were not paved with gold.

Soon rumors circulated of growing job opportunities in the industrial northern areas of New York State. The Erie Canal and the railroad system ran from New York City north along the Hudson River, made a turn westward at Albany and ran through Utica, Syracuse, Rochester, Schenectady and on to Buffalo on the edge of the Great Lakes. Industry was growing rapidly and needed cheap immigrant labor. The Mohawk Valley held a string of new factories making all manner of products. Gloves were made in Gloversville, silverware and china in Oneida, copper cookware in Rome, tools, fishing gear, rifles, beds, and furniture in Utica, film and cameras in Rochester. Fastest growing were a number of cotton mills which received bales of raw cotton from the southern states and converted them to sheets, pillow cases, carpets, towels, drapes and countless other everyday products for domestic and foreign markets. These mills created the need for many smaller support businesses and employment opportunities grew. Most of these cotton mills were clustered in and around Utica. Joseph, his common-law wife and three sons left Hamburg, again heading for a land of opportunity. For the unskilled there was plenty of work. Over the years that followed Nick did it all; cotton mills, laundries, coal yards, road work, pick and shovel. Like millions of immigrants his sweat built the roads, factories and wealth of a young nation.

Nick often remained barefoot in this land of reputed "plenty." When he found work that required foot protection, or during cold winter days, his father gave him his stepmother's worn out shoes to wear. Women shoe styles then had exaggerated, pointed toes. He broke the heels off and forced his feet into the shoes. Nick's toes were crushed together for long hours each day resulting in severe bunions that would plague him in later years.

Nick and his brother Bob were eligible to be drafted into the First World War conflagration. They, along with thousands of immigrants were drafted to fight for their new country. But Nick, thanks to his youth and severe bunions, was rejected, sparing him from the horror of trench and gas warfare in Europe. His brother, Bob, fought in Europe and returned apparently safe. However, his lungs were ravaged from mustard gas poisoning and a few years later he died from it.

One day Joseph received a letter from the authorities on Ellis Island saying his wife, Teresa Elia, had arrived and he needed to come and claim her. She had, indeed saved enough for passage to New York. He traveled to Ellis Island, met her, and with cold brutality declared that he did not know this woman. Since he already had a woman in his household he had no need for his legitimate wife, Teresa. One can only imagine her hurt and humiliation. She was returned to the ship and sailed back to Naples a few days later where she remained, alone, and struggled to survive.

Several years later, when his common-law wife died, Joseph sent Teresa money for passage to America. It was an act of practicality. Now he needed her.

Nick never forgave his father for this cruel act. Recalling it, years later, moved him to tears.

Nick's mother, Teresa Elia Manfredo. While I never knew her I came to love
her through the stories Dad told me.

THE COURTSHIP

In the summer of 1921 Bob Manfredo, Nick's oldest brother, returned from World War I. Bob had survived trench warfare in the fields of France and returned full of stories and a souvenir French bayonet. He also brought home an army buddy, Emilio Dinardi and introduced him to Nick. The three became good friends. When Emilio made plans to marry Nancy Giangolini he asked Nick to be his best man. Nancy had asked her youngest sister, Anna, to be the Maid of Honor. They told Nick he would accompany a pretty "Romana" a girl from Rome. After some coaxing Nick agreed as a favor to his friend. Nancy also assured a skeptical Anna that Nick was a nice young man and they would make a good looking couple.

They were a handsome couple and after the rehearsal the girls teased young Anna, asking if she found him attractive. She replied, with the biting impertinence of youth, "Well, he does have a handsome profile and what could pass for a Roman nose. I suppose if it is a hot day I can stand in its shade."

Nick was absolutely smitten. He moved in dreamlike slow motion during the wedding and the photo session that followed the wedding. She was a trim 5 foot 1 inch girl with dark brown eyes and hair and a mischievous personality. During the reception he sat in his assigned place at the head table, moving in a delirious trance all evening. They didn't miss a dance over the next six hours. Anna wondered, "What will people think?" Nick didn't care.

The next day Bob asked his little brother, "What did you think of her? You should ask her to be your girl." Nick replied, self deprecatingly, "A pretty girl like that wouldn't have someone like me." However, Nick visited Rotundo Photo Studios and bought a copy of the one wedding photo of him and Anna as Maid of Honor and Best Man. He wanted a picture showing himself and Anna as a couple. Mr. Rotundo said it could be done since he still had the negatives. A few days later Nick proudly carried the photo of himself and Anna as a couple. He could not wait to show it to Anna. Her response shocked him. This ever-so-proper young girl felt he had taken liberties with her image without her permission. They were not engaged, nor were they officially a couple. She felt violated and told him so. While this may seem strange in today's customs, in that day a girl would not approve of a boy carrying her photograph without her permission. Chastened thusly Nick was a miserable young man. He surrendered the photo to her.

Throughout the following weeks Nick managed to visit Anna's family in the company of Bob and Emilio and he grew more comfortable being in her presence. One evening, the two found themselves alone on the front porch, exchanging small talk. Nick had rehearsed the words a thousand times in his head. After much inner torture, he managed to say, "I have something to ask you. Will you be my girl?" She replied, "I don't know. You have to ask my parents,"

"What you want is all that matters," he said. She thought for a moment, and then added, "If my father approves it is alright with me."

The next Sunday morning, after church, Nick and his parents visited Anna and her family, a gallon of wine in hand. The parents talked. Nick's parents asked Anna's parents for approval. Anna's father, Augusto, asked her if this proposal was acceptable to her. She agreed it was. Then, after due consideration, Augusto gave his approval. Hands were shaken. Wine, coffee and biscotti were passed around.

Anna's parents, Maria and Augusto Giangolini, circa 1921.

As Nick and Anna sat on the porch that Sunday afternoon Anna said, "I have something for you," and unwrapping a handkerchief she lifted out the photograph he had reluctantly given to her weeks earlier. "This is yours now," she said. On the back she had written, in Italian, "To my Nicholas so my image is always in his mind!! Always think of me!! Your Anna. 9:20 AM, September 20, 1921"

They "kept company" from that day forward and were married the following spring at Saint Mary of Mount Carmel Church. They vowed to love, honor and cherish "until death do us part." In his last years he loved to tell the story of their courtship and when he reached the part where Anna and her father gave their approval he would add, with moist eyes, "And we were never apart again."

This photo of them as Best Man and Maid of Honor, taken at her sister Nancy's wedding, is the one Anna gave back to Nick on that Sunday after her parents gave permission for them to be engaged.

THE WEDDING NIGHT

Nicks knowledge of sex was drawn from what he had observed watching farm animals during his early years back in Italy. That knowledge was expanded by his male friends who were eager to educate him before his wedding. He had nothing remotely close to any actual experience.

Anna knew nothing about sex. As a little girl in Rome she and her sixteen year old girlfriend sometimes walked to Via Veneto and drank lemonades at a sidewalk table. One day Anna asked her friend why she was so sad. Her friend began to cry and said she had been "ruvenato" (ruined) by her boyfriend and her life was over. Not understanding Anna asked what the boyfriend had done. The girl said they had been "together." Seeing Anna's puzzled look she said, "It is like this glass. Now it is alright, but if I crack it, it will be ruined forever. That is what happened to me." Mom said, "Oh," still not comprehending. It wasn't until after her marriage that Dad explained to her what the girlfriend was trying to tell her.

During the days preceding the wedding there was much planning by the ladies about where Nick and Anna would live and how they would accommodate the needs that would arise when they eventually "bought a baby." That was the guarded expression commonly used to avoid divulging too much about the process to the young Italian women of that time.

Mom waited until she had a moment alone with her oldest sister, Nancy, and then asked where they should go to "buy a baby." Nancy told her they would have to order one from Woolworth's Department Store, the largest store in Utica, located at the "busy corner." The "busy corner" was a euphemism for the corner where Utica's two main streets, Bleecker and Genesee, intersected. So, on the day of her wedding Mom still believed that married couples purchased babies by placing an order at the largest department store in town.

My grandfather owned a two story home on the east side of Utica. Dad lived in a bedroom on the first floor of Grandpa's house. After the wedding reception the newlyweds retired, for the first time, to their room. The bedspread was covered with rice, confetti and money put there by the guests, as was the custom. They collected the rice and confetti—it is mounted around the old family photo shown on the front cover—and happily counted the money.

After individually and privately dressing for bed they lay, side by side, awkwardly talking. It wasn't long before Dad realized that his bride was totally naïve and was frightened by what he was suggesting. He held her and reassured her that he was happy just to be with her and they would make love when she felt ready to do so. It would be a number of days before Anna was ready. Meanwhile, they fell asleep in each other's arms for the first time.

The next morning they were greeted by family members in the hallway leading to their bedroom. Dad understood that his parents expected to perform the time honored, old country tradition of inspecting the bed sheets for signs that their son's bride had been a virgin. Of course, they would find no such proof since they had not consummated the marriage.

His parents moved toward the bedroom doorway. He stepped in front of them.

"Where are you going?" he asked.

They answered, "Per fara il costumo." To do the custom.

He looked them squarely in the eye, unmoving, and said, "What happens in our bedroom is between my wife and me and is no one else's business."

And that was the end of that.

Nick and Anna on their wedding day, April 22, 1922 at Saint Mary of Mount Carmel church, Utica, New York.

THE DEPRESSION YEARS

We lived in a third floor apartment with windows that looked down on Bleecker Street. A small recessed balcony with an iron railing opened onto our hall landing. In the summer we sat out there and watched the people and traffic below. Electric street cars growled by on steel wheels and rails, their spring-loaded antennas drawing power from electric cables overhead. Cars purred by.

On the fourth floor of the building across the street was Rossi Hall, a favorite location for Italian and Polish wedding receptions. The sounds of music and laughter often floated above the street at night. Night birds swooped after unseen bugs under starry skies. Sometimes, as little boys, we climbed up the fire escape stairs in the rear of Rossi Hall to wean pizza, kielbasa and soft drink handouts from the revelers. Winter drove us indoors where we leaned against window sills to watch people and vehicles now shrouded in snow and ice.

On summer days we often awoke to the cries of street vendors. "U' pizzaiollo," cried the pizza guy who carried a stack of wrapped, hot pizzas. "Rag-aza, rag-aza," was the call of the rag man whose horse drawn wagon held rags and scrap metal which he bought for pennies to resell at the salvage yards. "Verdzi, escarole, pomodori, ..." came from the driver of another horse drawn wagon heaped high with fruits and vegetables, a beam scale swinging from a hook on the side of the wagon.

As a baby I slept in a crib in my parents' large bedroom whose window overlooked the rooftop next door. It was out that window that Dad, exasperated by Mom's notorious nagging, flung his suit jacket out onto the snow covered roof and left it overnight. When tempers cooled the next morning he sheepishly climbed out to retrieve it and we all laughed as he carried in the jacket. It was frozen stiff, its' lapels standing awkwardly, sleeves askew as if flailing to cushion its' fall. It lay in the back room, on Mom's ironing board, until it thawed out and the arms slowly relaxed and gradually hung down on either side like a recovering drunk.

Each evening Dad read me a bedtime story while I looked out at him through the bars of my crib. His voice inflected the meanings and emotions of the words so well that I could imagine the characters of the story as if they were alive in my head.

By the time I was five years old I had moved into the front bedroom with my brother, Albert. Its' window faced Bleecker Street. At night Al and I would lie on our double bed in that front bedroom and fall asleep listening to the occasional passing car. As the faint hum of its motor grew louder a headlight beam climbed slowly up one wall. It grew to a crescendo as the beam crossed the ceiling. The light beam picked up speed crossing the ceiling and at the exact center of the ceiling the sound frequency suddenly dropped, the light rushed to the other wall and slowly crept down, light and sound growing fainter, then fading away to nothing. It was a soothing lullaby.

Dad had done pick and shovel work when it was available. He even delivered coal for a friend's coal yard, carrying heavy canvas bags of coal from the truck into back alleys where he dumped it into coal chutes shoved into cellar windows. He returned home, weary and black faced, flesh colored circles around his eyes. As the economic depression deepened jobs disappeared. Dad found work at the Hotel Martin, a four story brick edifice with a hundred or so rooms. He and a much older man ran the hotel laundry which was located in the cellar of the hotel. As a child I once accompanied Mom on a visit there to deliver a hot meal. We descended unlit stone stairs in the alley behind the hotel and opened a heavy wooden door. The large cellar had a dirt floor with concrete pads under the washing machines and dryers. A dim light came from naked bulbs hanging from the ceiling on thick, black wires. The air was dank and cloying, smelling of mold and musty wetness. The humidity was stifling. Two giant laundry tubs filled with steaming water held bedding, towels and table linens. Huge gas-fired hot water tanks kept the water at scalding temperature. Across from the washers were two large drying barrels fitted with oversized, hand fed roller wringers that squeezed most of the water out before tumbling the damp laundry. Hot air from gas heaters flowed through the laundry in the rotating barrels. At the far end of the cellar was a large, black, open pit filled with drainage from the tubs, still steaming and covered with soap scum. On the other side of the cellar stood a row of empty canvas carts waiting next to a freight elevator. We watched as Dad and the old man ran from tub to tub, alternately loading the washing machines, using wooden paddles to submerge the laundry between agitation blades, pulling armloads of wet laundry from the machines, hand feeding the wringers, then piling finished laundry in the carts. They moved continuously from operation to operation. The old man struggled to keep up. Dad often stopped what he was doing to lend a hand.

Dad sometimes brought home interesting things that were found in the dirty laundry as it arrived in the cellar. Paper umbrellas, fancy wooden and glass swizzle sticks, an occasional glass or spoon and once a small, white clay pipe left over from one of the many private dinner parties. These little pipes were occasionally served, along with powdered cocaine, at private parties. It was considered an exotic, but harmless social drug back then. I still have that pipe, carefully wrapped and locked in a metal storage box.

Dad and the old man worked six nights a week. He came home around midnight, washed, ate, and then went to bed, arising mid-morning. Each night they washed the day's laundry and stayed until the last of it was put into the canvas wheeled carts to be taken up the freight elevators. The shift lasted about 10 hours depending on the amount of laundry. They were each paid a flat $7 per week for 60 plus hours. The depression was in full swing. They felt lucky to have jobs.

One night, as they were ready to leave, the boss told them that the hotel could no longer afford two men in the laundry room. They let the old man go. They said Dad could stay if he agreed to do the job alone in return for which they would give him an extra $2 a week. It meant $9 for a week that averaged 80 hours. He felt sorry for the old man but had to accept the offer.

Business continued to decline. A few months later the hotel closed the laundry and sent what little laundry they had to an outside service. Dad was sent home. Many of our friends and neighbors were similarly unemployed. They went daily to stand in bread lines which grew longer each week. Dad would not go. It would have shamed him to accept what he considered charity.

George Flemma owned a small shoe store in the building next door. Dad had helped him from time to time with projects around the store. He remembered that an old, broken two seat shoe shine stand was collecting dust and cob webs in the stores' basement. He asked George if he could borrow it. He offered to repair, clean and paint it and return it in good condition. Mr. Flemma agreed. After that, while others went to the bread lines every morning, Dad shined shoes on the corner of Bleecker and Mohawk Streets. Albert helped on weekends. As a little boy I could only watch and keep them company when things were slow.

A long time family friend, Tony, the milkman, owned the Blue Ribbon Dairy, located just outside the city of Utica. Tony made deliveries with a horse drawn milk wagon, often before dawn. The horse knew each delivery location on his route and stopped at the curb without being told. A long leather strap was permanently attached to the horses' bridle. The other end was tied to an iron weight resting on the step of the wagon. Tony would lower the weight to the street which served to hitch the horse in place. It waited patiently for Tony to return, chewing lazily on the contents of the canvas nose bag strapped over its' muzzle.

Tony would walk up to the second floor landing where we left our empties. He'd read the note Mom had tucked into one of the empty bottles. It told him how many fresh quarts to leave. He would pull that many out of his metal basket, pick up the empties and return to the wagon. The horse would start walking just as Tony lifted the weight and placed one foot on the wagon step.

Each bottle showed a naked baby wrapped in a large blue ribbon bearing the words, "Keep me cool, I'll keep sweet!" and under that, "BLUE RIBBON DAIRY." The bottles had small, round cardboard caps pressed into the bottle tops. On winter mornings the cream at the top would freeze and expand, lifting the cap up. When Al and I awoke we would race down to the second floor landing to get the milk and, if the cream was frozen we'd steal a taste of the "ice cream" before Mom scooped it off and saved it for coffee or cooking.

Very early one morning, shortly after Dad lost his job at the hotel, there was a knock at our door. Mom and I were up. Al was in the bathroom getting ready for school. I followed Mom to the door. There stood Tony, the milkman. In one hand was his metal basket full of quarts of fresh milk. In the other he held Mom's note.

"What does this mean?" he asked. Mom looked embarrassed and told him that Dad was out of work and we could not afford to buy milk for a while.

"What am I supposed to do with this milk?" he asked, holding up his full basket. "If I take it back to the dairy it will only spoil. I'll leave milk every delivery, like always. Some day you will pay me what you owe. I know I can trust you. The boys need their milk." And without another word he walked into the kitchen, pulled the full quarts from his basket, set them on the table, reached down his hand to muss my hair, and left. I ran to the window and watched him step up into the already moving milk wagon. I didn't understand, then, why Mom's eyes were filled with tears.

I don't know how long it was before we were able to pay Tony, but he never missed a delivery. Not once.

Dad shined shoes for a long time until, one day, he learned that the cotton mills were getting large military orders and were hiring. He applied and was hired. He returned the shoe shine stand to the store basement and resumed steady work at one of the mills. The pay envelopes started to arrive regularly and slowly things began to look promising.

One of the first bills he paid was to Tony, the milkman.

RECOVERY

We listened to President Roosevelt stumping for re-election on our Philco Super Hetrodyne Radio. The world was troubled by what was happening in Europe and the Far East. Roosevelt's opponents were suggesting that his administration would lead us into World War II. "I promise you again and again and again, your sons shall not set foot on foreign soil," he intoned. Meanwhile cotton mills, gun factories and other critical manufacturers were gearing up to supply countries like Britain and France in their struggle against Germany, Italy and Japan. Our Pacific Fleet carried a big stick to hold Japan at arm's length. Roosevelt was re-elected.

Japan attacked the United States Pacific naval fleet at Pearl Harbor on December 7, 1941 and, almost simultaneously, declared war on the United States. Roosevelt and congress declared war on Japan. The German – Italian axis declared war on the United States. We declared back. World War II was on.

The economic recovery of the United States went into high gear as factories tooled up and hired all the able bodied people they could find. Dad worked long hours at the cotton mill. Albert graduated from high school and immediately entered the toolmaker apprenticeship program at Savage Arms, a manufacturer of rifles, machine guns and other wartime weapons.

With two incomes and much commuting Albert begged the folks to buy a car. He had a friend who was selling a beautiful 1939 two door Pontiac convertible sports car, garnet red exterior, black leather interior, ivory steering wheel and knobs, white canvas top with two, fold-down jump seats behind the two front seats. After much anguish they bought the car for $600. Rationing hit us almost immediately. Our gasoline ration window sticker was for the minimal amount of gasoline since we didn't have a high priority need to use the car. Detroit stopped producing passenger cars and started making war machines; tanks, trucks, jeeps, airplane parts. At least once a week we received offers to buy our car at double what we had paid. There were no new cars available.

Mom never could understand that the car was an inanimate machine and did not have a life of its own. That first winter the folks rented a garage and Mom insisted that on cold nights Dad go cover the hood with a blanket. Infrequently we took weekend trips to visit friends or churches in nearby villages. None was more than 15 miles away. After each such trip Mom would not permit use of the car for at least a week, "To let it rest."

Our first car, a garnet 1939 Pontiac convertible purchased after the start of WW II, parked in front of the apartment building where Al and I grew up.

Albert was drafted into the army almost a year after the declaration of war. I remember that rainy day. We drove him, in the car he so loved, to the railroad station. Utica's railroad station was a massive structure of marble and granite, constructed at a time when state politicians thought Utica was going to be the new state capital. That never happened and the station was usually quiet. It was teeming now with shipments of people and goods. But that cold, wet, early morning it was empty except for a few young men who, like Albert, stood in small groups with their families, waiting for the train that would take them to Fort Dix, New Jersey. After basic training he was sent to Fort Ord in California. Then he shipped out of San Francisco to somewhere in the Pacific theater of operations.

Mom prepared packages for him, addressed to strange post offices. We never knew for sure where he was. They contained food and letters and sometimes pictures. We received a small flag to hang in our window which showed that we had a loved one in the service. Her packages and letters flowed to Albert until the day he returned home. Tear stained letters followed him across the United States and Pacific Ocean.

The start of World War II changed many things. Since Italy was one of our enemies all Italians who had not yet achieved citizenship were labeled foreign or enemy aliens. This carried an unpleasant stigma. Dad had achieved citizenship in 1926. Mom wanted dearly to become an American citizen. Late in the war she began taking evening classes in English and citizenship. She learned the fundamentals of our government and memorized the pledge of allegiance in English.

Part of her final test included an oral exam. The examiner asked her what she had done to support the war effort. She could have said she had provided a son, Albert, who was serving in the United States Army. Instead she replied, shyly, that she had put grease on the curbstone. After a puzzled pause the examiner realized what she meant and smiled. Kitchen grease was used to manufacture explosives. Citizens were urged to save used kitchen grease in bottles or cans and set them out on the curb for weekly pickup. That is what Mom did. She earned her citizenship in April, 1944.

On graduation day she posed for a class photo proudly clutching her certificate of citizenship. She framed and kept it on display in our little living room for many years.

Mom's graduation class photo, front row, second from the left. She became a proud citizen of the United States April, 1944.

Mom was a great cook. I loved all her food, but I could not bring myself to eat the drumsticks of her delicious roast chicken because I could see the tiny blood vessels that coursed through the dark meat. So, to her consternation, I picked drumstick meat apart trying to separate out the tiny blood vessels— until World War II.

There were frequent night time air raid drills along the eastern seaboard during World War II. When sirens went off we immediately extinguished all lights. Air raid wardens prowled the streets looking for any trace of house lights. One night the sirens sounded just as Mom removed roast chicken from the oven and set it on the table. We quickly doused all lights and sat in a pitch black kitchen. We could see nothing. The room filled with a delicious aroma of roast chicken and vegetables. We tried to wait for the all clear siren but hunger got the best of us. Mom suggested we try to eat in the dark. Groping, we tore chunks off the bird. I grabbed a drumstick certain that I would taste the veins and be able to pick them out. To my surprise, I reached a leg bone and tasted only the succulent dark meat. I never fussed over chicken again. I was cured by a mock air raid, and hunger.

The government urged citizens to grow their own food. George Flemma purchased several acres on the outskirts of Utica which he planned to farm. His friendship with Dad led him to ask for his help in return for a share of the crops. It was a chance to supplement our food supply. We grew all manner of vegetables, Dad doing the lion's share of the work. Evenings and weekends, when he wasn't working, he rode his bike to the lots and tilled the soil, planted, weeded, watered, fertilized and harvested. He often took me along for company, riding on the crossbar of his bike. The Reverend Vincent Gottuso told us he could find a location to dig a well. He came out one weekend, cut a Y shaped branch from a particular tree and used it as a divining rod to find a good place to dig a well. He walked back and forth across the acreage holding the top of the Y tightly in his fists, the stem pointing forward. From time to time the rod twisted downward and finally pointed straight down at a low lying spot half way down the slightly sloping lots. We dug there and about six feet down we hit sweet, cool water. We removed mud until we had two or three feet of standing water. Since the water tables around Utica were fairly high we would probably have hit water any place we dug, but there it was, our own water supply. We used a bucket tied on a rope, tossed in and hauled out by hand.

Mom packed meals for us, often a large plate of pasta with sauce and meats. Dad managed to balance me on the bicycle crossbar and I held the pasta. We usually did not carry utensils. When we broke for lunch he cut two small branches from a nearby tree, shaped like three-tinned forks, and sharpened them with his pocket knife. We pulled fresh green onions from the ground, munched on tomatoes and cucumbers off the vine. With an occasional hot pepper and cool water from the well we ate and drank like kings.

After each harvest Mom and Dad spent many hours canning vegetables which they stored in the cellar beneath the apartment building. Once a year, in the winter, they bought a slab of pork and made sausage which they air dried in an unheated, frigid room and bottled in olive oil.

We supplemented our food supply another way. In the fall we went hunting for mushrooms in woods outside Utica. These, too, were cooked and canned. Dad knew many that were safe. When we picked questionable ones Mom would boil these separately with a silver dollar in the water. The belief was that the silver would tarnish if the mushrooms were deadly. It did happen now and then.

Dad and I would go together, then split up and meet at a distant landmark. He carried a hand held compass to keep us from getting lost. If George went with us we would drive farther, to deeper woods and cover longer distances. Mom would come with us but remain with the car which was parked out on a meadow or dirt trail at the edge of the woods. At a pre-arranged time she would blow the horn at five minute intervals so we could all find our way back.

She packed a lunch for us. Sometimes we carried a cooler with steaks and condiments and at noon we made a fireplace out of stones. At George's insistence we would slip into a nearby farmers fields and steal fresh corn and potatoes to cook with our steaks. We were careful to avoid being seen. We buried the potatoes and corn in the ground beneath the firewood, before lighting it. The steaks were cooked in hand held wire baskets, over the flames. As the crackling fire heated the stones moisture trapped inside them would turn to steam and sometimes cause them to explode, much to my delight. By the time the steaks were cooked the potatoes and corn were baked and ready to dig out.

Late in the afternoon, on our way home, George would drive to the farmhouse, ask the farmer how much he would charge for what we took, and pay him. One day I asked him why he didn't pay the farmer first so we didn't have to sneak around the back edge of the field and "steal" it. He smiled and said, "It tastes better this way." I think he was right.

One cold, fall day, while crossing over an ice cold stream over a fallen log, I slipped and filled both boots with ice water. I had no extra set of dry socks and thought it would be the end of my hunting day. Dad calmly emptied my boots, removed my socks, wrapped old newspapers around my feet and put my boots back on me. My feet were toasty warm. He was my hero.

Starting out another morning he told me to cross a small stream and check out a large fallen log for mushrooms, and then continue on an easterly heading to a hilltop several miles distant which was visible above the trees. He was going to head south, downstream a mile, cut across and meet me on that hill. He started south. I slid down the embankment and rock-stepped across the stream carrying my basket and wearing a hunting knife for cutting mushrooms. I checked one side of the log and found no mushrooms. I stepped on the log to leap to the other side and my boot crashed through the rotten wood. I extracted it and continued over the log. Something landed on my forehead, clinging tenaciously. I thought it was a dry leaf and plucked it away, but not before it stung me. I looked at my hand and saw I held pieces of a yellow jacket. I had crushed their hive with my boot. They were all over me before I knew what was happening. I yelled and ran back across the stream, clawing at the steep, muddy embankment on hands and knees, my head surrounded by angry yellow jackets. Dad came running, pulled a young tree out by the roots and used it to fend off the yellow jackets so I could gain footing and climb over the embankment. I ran for a long time.

I was wearing several pairs of old shirts and pants to protect against the frosty autumn cold. They had holes in them but the holes did not overlap each other so I was warm. But the yellow jackets found the holes and crawled in. The main hive had stopped following me but the ones already inside my clothes kept stinging. Dad finally caught up with me and began killing yellow jackets that were crawling between the layers of clothing. We could see them moving under the clothes. Using his cap he crushed them. With each one crushed I was stung again. That night I ran a fever, but it passed. Dad was my hero, again.

Albert returned safely from the war and went to work at the new Chicago Pneumatic Tool Company. The family was once again whole and prosperous. Life was good.

SIN CITY

The construction of the Erie Canal through the small city of Utica, New York, stimulated industrial development. This marvel of engineering led to the construction of dozens of cotton mills in the late 1800s and early 1900s. The creation of jobs attracted immigrants from Europe, mainly Italian, Irish and Polish.

By the late 1920s two political leaders emerged as the seats of political power; Rufus P. Elephante who controlled the Italian votes and Charles Donnelly who controlled the Irish vote. In 1928 they formed a coalition that created an unbeatable powerhouse for the Democratic Party. It held massive political clout and eventually used it to help put Theodore Roosevelt into the White House. Rosario Mancuso, Joseph and Salvadore Falcone were alleged to be a part of this powerful machine.

By the 1940s prostitution and gambling was rampant in Utica. The organization boasted mafia chieftains whose names struck fear in the citizenry. My brother and I attended school with the children of these families.

During those years over a dozen gangland murders in Utica were alleged to have ties to the Mafia organization. It was known among the Italians as Il Mano Nero, a Sicilian carryover of The Black Hand. But more frequently it was called Il Sindico; The

Syndicate. It was later popularized as La Cosa Nostra, or Our Thing. Utica became known as the sin city of the Mohawk Valley. It was the syndicates' Camelot.

A young man who crossed the wrong people was found one morning hanging from a street lamp. Another was invited to meet with them one Sunday afternoon to make peace. He was instructed to be outside the Eagle Brewery at 2 PM. He and his family attended early Mass and ate a sumptuous lunch. As he left for the rendezvous his sister, brother and a visiting cousin offered to walk with him, for the exercise, they said. They reached the appointed corner and the relatives turned to walk back home. A car slowed and stopped. Machine gun fire killed them all. Il Sindico could not afford to leave witnesses.

Two weeks later, as Dad and I walked past the brewery he showed me the bullet holes in the bricks of the Eagle Brewery. I recall reaching out and putting my fingers into them. They were there years later when I visited Utica from college.

The owner of the Ace of Clubs, located just across the street from Proctor Park, was gunned down one night after he closed the club. He was walking to the mail box on the corner. He had somehow alienated the syndicate. My school buddies and I heard about it the next day and as we left Proctor High School we went out of our way to walk past the Ace of Clubs. We stopped to look at the mailbox on the street corner. There was nothing to see, just a mailbox and a gravel parking lot. But our imaginations recreated it all.

One school chum, a big bruiser named Al, had particularly close ties to the Mafia. Al sold football pool tickets and took bets at school. One day he told me he was selling tickets to a stag party. He promised food, drink, hostesses and pornographic movies. Several of my more prosperous friends had already bought tickets. Others began saving up. A few weeks later he returned their money and told them it had been cancelled. When I pressed him for a reason he looked cautiously around then whispered, "Dewey is coming."

Thomas E. Dewey had earned a reputation as a "Gangbuster" while he was a special prosecutor for the borough of Manhattan in New York City. He was now Governor of New York State and seeking re-election. His "secret" raid was one in a series designed to ferret out Mafia corruption and enhance his re-election. Dewey and his boys showed up about two weeks later. According to headlines several criminal underlings were arrested and prosecuted. Clearly, however, the syndicate knew well in advance of the "secret" raid and arranged to toss Dewey a few harmless bones. Such was the influence of the syndicate network.

The older syndicate members hung out at local coffee shops where they enjoyed small cups of very sweet, black coffee in demitasse cups and puffed on strong, black cigars while playing cards and discussing business. Two favorite hangouts—preferred by the younger members— were Mutz's Drug Store and an ice cream parlor called The Mellow Shop located at the corner of Bleecker and Mohawk Streets. These were almost directly across the street from the buildings we lived in.

Three doors west of our building, on Bleecker Street, was Farina's Meat Market. It had a full basement which often served as a meeting place for the chieftains. During the meat rationing days of World War II the lights in that basement burned all night as illicit beef was cut up for the black market. On some nights the lights indicated a meeting of the "capi," the heads of the syndicate.

We lived in the safest part of town. Despite the violence and fear in the city we knew no incidents would ever be permitted in that part of Utica.

On warm summer evenings in the 1940s my parents and I would sometimes sit in the family car, parked in a driveway behind our building because it was cooler than our upstairs apartment. The car windows were open and we enjoyed the peacefulness of the starlight. This driveway opened onto Mohawk Street which was unlit. It cut behind our building and into the back yards of the next few buildings. Through this driveway one could walk, unseen all the way, through unfenced back yards to the back door of the basement below Farina's Meat Market.

I recall several dark nights when, as we sat in our car, two men came walking down the driveway from Mohawk Street. They stopped, one on each side of the car. Mom and Dad were in the front seat. I sat in the rear. They leaned slightly to look into the open windows and, recognizing our family, tipped their hats and said, in gentle Italian, "Good evening Mr. Manfredo, Mrs. Manfredo. Hello Joey. It is a beautiful night isn't it? Are you enjoying the air?"

Then one of them asked how my brother, Albert, was and my parents told him of the latest letters we had received from Albert who was stationed somewhere in the Pacific Theater of war operations. After a while, they wished us a good evening, tipped their hats again and nodded to someone at the end of the driveway. They stood aside as several dark figures walked past our car and on to Farina's basement. They tipped their hats as they passed. We knew who they were but no one spoke their names.

During those years we briefly lived in a rear apartment on the second floor of the building that housed the Flemma Shoe Store. To reach our small apartment from Bleecker Street you walked down a long, narrow alley from Bleecker Street to the back door at the rear end of the building. Just beyond the back door the alley intersected the driveway that came from Mohawk Street. When Dad was transferred from the day shift to swing shift he did not get home until 11:00 PM. He walked that long alley every night. Mom or I would go down the back stairs after sunset and flip on the inside switch. It lit the light over the back alley door so Dad could see his way.

One night Dad came home to find the light out. He stepped into the hallway and toggled the wall switch but the light did not work. He pulled a wooden crate from the hallway and stood on it, intending to change the light bulb. The bulb was only loose.

He tightened it. A week or so later he came home to find it out again. He tightened it, again, before coming upstairs. A week later it happened again.

The next day, as Dad was leaving for work, one of the syndicate soldiers approached him. After pleasantries the man very nicely told Dad that "they" would appreciate it if he would refrain from tightening the loose light bulb until the following day, "Come favore." As a favor.

Suddenly it was clear. On those nights the bulb had been unscrewed because one or more of the "capi" was attending a meeting and did not want to be an easy target while walking to and from Farina's Market.

Indeed, we lived in the safest part of town.

OTTER LAKE

I spent the summer of 1942 at beautiful Otter Lake, high in the Adirondack Mountains about 30 miles north of Utica, New York. Church friends of my parents had asked if I could spend the summer with their son, Vincent, at their summer camp at Otter Lake.

Vincent was a good looking 25 year old who stayed year round at their cottage, spending days on a Chris Craft motorboat, lying on the deck, in the middle of the lake, absorbing the sunshine and occasionally coughing and spitting into tissues which he carefully bagged to be burnt on the weekends when his family came to the camp to visit. Vinny was dying of tuberculosis. Rest and long days in the sun were believed to be helpful in fighting this often incurable disease. He longed for company and I was to be his companion that summer.

During the week, when Vinny felt well enough, we'd take the 18 foot Chris Craft power boat out of the boat house, drive around the lake a while, then turn off the engine in the middle of the lake. He would lie on the deck for hours, absorbing sunshine, reading or sleeping, while I played with a fishing rod or swam or read. Sometimes we'd take it to the dock near the center of the village and go ashore to buy something at the little general store or the drug store. Once Vinny felt confident in my ability he sometimes let me go fetch the boat alone and drive it to the village dock where he would be waiting with our towels and picnic basket. Each weekend his family members, his beautiful fiancé and my parents came up to visit. They stayed overnight in the main house. My bedroom was a small room over the garage. I was 10 years old.

Vincent was a medical student and contracted his disease just before graduating from medical school. The main house was full of medical books and I spent some time looking through them. Vinny delighted in answering my questions. He was an intelligent young man and enjoyed having someone to banter with. One reference book caught my attention because of its title; "The Physiological Basis of Therapeutics." I asked him what that meant and he explained. I thought the title sounded neat and would recite it to impress my friends.

In the woods, at the edge of the lake, stood a beautiful brick summer home with a sizable boat house and power boat. It belonged to one of Utica's most notorious and feared mafia chiefs. His son, Joseph Junior, was my age.

When Vincent and I weren't out on the boat I hung out with Junior. We fished off the docks, catching small sunfish and releasing them. We played at the large fountain in the small town square, sometimes catching frogs that lived in the fountain. Junior discovered that if he threw them up in the air and let them hit the pavement a long, pink tongue would loll out and wouldn't retract until the frog regained consciousness. On occasion he threw one too high and the tongue never retracted. We hid these in the woods.

In the evening we hung around the big tourist Inn to see what important people might be there. Otter Lake was one of a string of lakes in the Adirondacks that attracted many big name entertainers. One night we peeked into the lounge and witnessed Kate Smith of God Bless America fame, with her manager, sitting at the bar. We recognized him from his television appearances with Kate Smith. She seemed drunk and was making a scene. We giggled and scratched when, in a rage, she cursed him out and whacked him with her large purse.

One day Junior and I had a disagreement which escalated to a shoving match and finally to blows. We exchanged some pretty stiff punches and I was surprised when Junior began to cry. His lament grew louder and then he said the awful words, "I'm gonna tell my Father!" I considered this a death threat.

I tried to calm him down, to divert his intent, to keep him from carrying out his threat. He soon realized that I was terrified and this emboldened him. He walked purposefully down the road, ignoring my pleas. He turned off the road taking a short cut through the woods. I could see his house just ahead by the lake.

I said something apologetic; the exact words escape me now. His crying grew louder as we approached the house. The door flew open and the dreaded Mafioso chieftain stepped out on the raised brick porch wearing black, pin stripped pants and matching vest over an open collared white shirt. His rolled up sleeves revealed broad wrists above half closed fists. Junior ran up the several brick steps, sobbing. His father scowled and barked, "What's the matter?" Juniors' crying increased and in a stricken voice he whined, "Joey hit me!!"

I knew I was a dead boy. The people of Utica spoke this man's name in whispers. I thought of running but knew that would only postpone the inevitable retribution that would surely follow. There was no place to hide. It seemed best to accept it now and get it over with.

Powerless, I looked up at the fathers' frowning face as he slowly and deliberately asked me, "Did you hit him?"

Better to die bravely, I thought.

"Yes!" I said through teeth clenched to keep them from chattering, "And I'd do it again!"

Joseph Senior gazed down at me intently. Then he half turned and cuffed Junior sharply on the back of his head. "You must've deserved it," he said. "Get in the house."

Junior looked startled. I must have looked astounded, or at least relieved. The door closed behind them.

As I walked back through the woods and then down the road I felt wonderment that this Mafia Chieftain had behaved exactly as my own parents would have in the same circumstance. They would have given the benefit of the doubt to the other guy. And I would have learned, as I am sure Junior did, that it was better to resolve my own misadventures without involving my parents for they would surely assume that I was at fault. And, right or wrong, it would eventually make us more independent and self reliant.

I knew very well the types of crimes this man was alleged to have committed against society. I did not doubt they were true. Yet, from that day on, to me he was just another Italian father.

At the end of summer residents and weekend visitors began closing down their cabins for the winter months. One by one, acquaintances said goodbye and drove down the mountain road to the city. On the last weekend I prepared to leave. Vincent would remain through the winter. My bags were packed. When my folks arrived Mom gave me a beautiful white suit with white shirt, tie and shoes and told me to put them on for our last big meal with Vincent's family. I dressed, and then found dinner would not be ready for a while, so I wandered down the main road promising to be back in an hour. Mom warned me to be careful and stay clean.

I arrived at the cabin of another little friend whose family kept chickens in the yard. Since they would be gone all winter they decided to butcher the three or four chickens that remained and pack the meat home. I was fascinated. My little friend and I stood back and watched as his Dad chopped off their heads and threw the flopping bodies to the ground. The birds took a while to die and flung themselves, blindly, about the yard. I felt something running down my cheek. I wiped it away and looked at my hand. It was covered with blood. Then I saw the look of horror on my friends face. He was staring, open mouthed, at my suit. I looked down and saw red polka dots on my white tie, shirt, jacket, pants and shoes. I tried to wipe them away only to smear the larger drops.

This was one of those times when I was certain that the fate which awaited me at the hands of my Mother was going to be awful. With a heavy heart and a gut full of dread I walked back to our cabin. Mom saw me coming through the windows of the sun porch and came out to meet me. She took it all in with a slow head to toe look. I said something about the family down the road killing their chickens. Then she did what sometimes surprised me so much. With profound gentleness and understanding she simply said, "Go wash up and change into something clean and come to dinner." And that was all I ever heard about it.

We ate dinner leisurely with all of Vinny's family and his fiancé. After our goodbyes we drove down the mountain and returned home. It had been a long, grand summer for a 10 year old.

I wrote to Vinny a few times. He answered me with long, thoughtful letters which, I knew, he had treated with ultraviolet rays before sending them. He was meticulously careful to avoid infecting others with his disease. Over the next year or so we kept informed about Vinny's progress through his sister, Rosie Mancuso, a close friend of Mom's.

Vincent died the next year.

THE COTTON MILLS

I stared into the dark shadows at the rear corner of the empty freight car in the direction my father was pointing. There, in the sweltering gloom, crouched in one corner, was a miniature monster. It was shaped like a frog with a large head, its fat, grayish body covered with what looked like small spikes. Two horny ridges over its eyes looked like menacing eyebrows or evil horns. Its bowed legs tensed and its body swelled as I neared to get a better look. I had never seen anything like it and my fourteen year old mind was fascinated.

"That's a horned toad," Dad said. "It must've got in the freight car when they were loading cotton down south. It's really a lizard." We were standing inside an empty freight car on the railroad tracks that stood next to the cotton mill loading docks.

Dad usually carried his lunch to the mill when he left for work but, for some reason which I would understand much later, he suggested to Mom that I take lunch to him that day. I rode my bike over Bleecker Street, then down Mohawk Street a number of blocks to the outskirts of town. I approached the long rows of brick buildings which constituted the cotton mills. They hummed with the sounds of machines. Around the back were railroad tracks. Parked on them were half a dozen freight cars, most still loaded with tightly stacked cotton bales. Rows of cotton bales rested on the loading dock.

I leaned the bike against the side of the stairs leading up to the loading platform. I walked up and peered into the building through the immense, roll-up steel doors that, when open, made a wide gaping entrance to the mill. A piercingly loud whistle blew for several seconds. Men strolled past me carrying lunch pails, chattering while they sought a shady part of the loading dock or sat in the open doorways of the freight cars.

Dad appeared, wiping sweat from his brow. He was wearing grey cotton work pants, a white, sleeveless undershirt and a grey cotton cap. I handed him the lunch pail and thermos filled with a coffee and milk mixture. This Italian "caffe e latte," or coffee and milk, is today commonly called "latte" and sells for $6.00 a cup. Back then Mom made it by boiling milk and adding it to hot coffee, then filling the thermos.

We sat apart from the others. He gave me the extra sandwich Mom had made for me and poured a little of the caffe e latte into the thermos cap for me. He drank from the thermos. We ate together in silence.

When we were done eating he rose and said, "Do you want to see what we do here?"

"You bet," I said eagerly.

He closed the lunch pail and strapped it to my bike again.

Dad took me first into the freight cars and explained how the cotton was baled and stuffed into them for shipment to the mills that populated upstate New York. Literally dozens of cotton mills were located in this area; known since the late 1800's as the textile center of the United States.

Then we entered the back of the mill. The air was hot and sultry and laden with dust. Machines stood in long lines, driven by wide leather belts looped over long, ceiling mounted drive shafts. A large electric motor at the far end of each shaft drove it via a wide leather belt drive. The noise was overpowering.

Sweating, bare-chested men heaved and clawed at the cotton,

expertly avoiding being caught and drawn into the machines. Millwrights, who repaired and maintained the machines, did so with machines running whenever possible to keep production up. My father was a millwright. He showed me some of his tools and how they were used to repair broken drive belts or make other repairs by disengaging or changing the gear pulleys without turning off the motors. There was a certain pride in the way he showed me what he did and how the processes worked. The danger was obvious. I noticed several workers with missing digits and one with a missing hand. Dad showed me where those type of accidents had happened. He had witnessed some of them. He had come close to being in one of them.

He explained each operation as we slowly walked through, stopping now and then to watch men struggling with the cotton as it made its way through the machines. I watched them cut the bales free, and feed them into the bale breakers where they were torn apart with large, rotating steel-spiked drums. From time to time the cotton jammed up and one or two workers leapt forward, reached in with rakes, poles or their hands to break it loose, drums and spikes rotating relentlessly.

The cotton moved to blowers for cleaning and drying. Other machines performed a "willowing" operation. He explained "breaking scutches" and "batting," "finishing scutches" and "lapping." The resulting "staples" were moved to the carding room where the carding machines, which looked like giant, dog-grooming steel brushes, straightened out the staples and combed them into "roving."

In the spinning room machines made the roving into yarn, then processed the yarn into thread. The thread was wound rapidly onto large, tapered spools, shuttles and bobbins. On we went past the spinning mills, into the weaving mill room. Workers, many of them women, tended huge looms. Each operator was responsible for 4 to 6 looms. The slapping and clatter of the shuttles, bobbins, beaters and warping boards in the looms was deafening.

The pace was frantic, the room hot and gloomy. Dusty light filtered through the dirty, steel framed industrial windows mounted high in the walls, close to the ceiling. Workers hurried to keep pace with the machines, repairing, re-threading, loading, unloading. Everywhere people scurried, hair pasted to foreheads with perspiration, clothing clinging wetly. Faces wore a patina of sweat streaked dust.

I shouted over the noise to Dad, saying that they must welcome winter for relief from the heat. He pointed to steam pipes that lined the ceiling. He said the mill was maintained at 100 degrees Fahrenheit in the winter because it helped the process. Even in winter there was no relief from the heat and humidity.

The cotton dust caused bronchitis and tuberculosis. The thumping of the 500 looms at 200 times per minute led to premature deafness. Lubricants used on the machines were later found to be carcinogenic and led to cancer of the mouth and scrotum, a malady known to the workers commonly as "mule-spinners disease."

This was the Mohawk Cotton Mill in Utica. Its' employees lived and shopped wherever they pleased or could afford. But other mills were more captive.

Not far away was the small town of New York Mills. It contained three huge cotton mills, each one much larger than the one we were in. New York Mills was a complete company town which provided employment along with company owned housing and stores. Those who worked in New York Mills usually rented housing from the mill and purchased all their needs at company stores which offered food, clothing and other family necessities. The weekly pay came as cash in small, brown manila envelopes. Notated on the outside of each envelope, in pencil, was the employees name and an accounting of how much had been earned, how much rent, grocery and merchandise expense was deducted during that week and the balance to be found inside the envelope. It was seldom more than a few dollars. Employees with large families sometimes owed more than they made and went home with empty envelopes now and then.

We walked back toward the loading docks, my lungs aching for clean, cooler air, my ears ringing from the noise. As we reached the back doors Dad's boss came up to us. He asked who I was, then told Dad that it was against the rules for non-workers, especially kids, to be inside the mill. He admonished Dad gently but with serious concern. Dad said he understood and it wouldn't happen again.

"Did you know I wasn't supposed to be inside?" I asked, once we were outside again.

"Sure," he said. He put a hand on my shoulder and said, "Joey, I wanted you to see how I make a living. If you don't study hard and get a good education you could end up in a place like this. I didn't have the opportunity to go to school when I was growing up, but you do."

We stood quietly on the loading dock for another minute. He lowered his hand. I walked down the steps and got on my bike. He turned once before he re-entered the cotton mill and our eyes met. Then he was gone. The strident whistle blew again. I rode home deep in thought. Dad had never spoken to me about education before. He never mentioned it again. But I never forgot it.

Dad had taught us, by example, that there is no shame in hard work and the importance of taking pride in doing the best you can in any endeavor. But today was different. Someone once wrote that the most forceful messages are delivered, not by pronouncements, but by telling a story that leads the listener to draw their own, inevitable conclusion. In his own way my unschooled father told me a story that day. Its message was received and it profoundly influenced my life.

GOING TO COLLEGE

It was 1950. I was a senior at Thomas R. Proctor High School in upstate New York. All my school chums were talking about their plans after graduation. Some had already been accepted by colleges.

Joe Hobika was going to become a dentist. Sammy Scotellaro would become a CPA. Anthony (Chickie) La Porte, my best friend, was undecided. He might go to work for Wolf News, a magazine distributor where his father worked. Rocco S. would become a lawyer and a major political power in Albany, New York, the State Capital. Felix Rotundo would become a professional photographer and probably take over his father's photo shop one day. Joe Spano would continue working for his father who owned the Ohio Bakery. He would eventually inherit and operate the bakery. Joe was one of the few kids in our school who had his own car. Salvatore Buttiglieri would become an insurance salesman like his Father. Salvatore Viti wasn't sure, yet, but figured to get a job at one of the local businesses. What he lacked in grades he made up for in charisma. He would eventually become First Shift General Foreman in the local General Electric Plant. Anthony Ruggiero planned to continue working in his Father's hat store, selling and cleaning men's hats. He would eventually own it. Anthony had to wear a man's felt dress hat to high school every day to promote his father's business. Hank Maggiore would become an auto mechanic, and a good one.

I wanted to go to college but wasn't sure what profession to pursue. It didn't matter because my family could not afford to pay for college nor did they favor what they perceived as collegiate un-Godliness. So, when the time came to elect a high school major I did not take the college preparatory curriculum. Instead, I majored in technical tool making, as had my brother, nine years before me. I planned to apply for a job as an apprentice toolmaker at the old Savage Arms factory or the new Chicago Pneumatic Tool factory which had just been opened on the outskirts of town. My brother was already working at the latter as a journeyman toolmaker.

As the end of the year approached the Boy's Counselor, Mr. Huff, scheduled each graduating senior for private counseling. When I told him my plans he asked if I had considered college. I said, as my brother did nine years earlier, that my family could not afford it. I did not tell him that my parents were strict fundamentalist Christians, unsophisticated, good people who mistrusted the world and its evils.

My Mother's position was unequivocal. She spoke to me in Italian because her English was broken and she wanted to be perfectly clear. "You will not go away to college and do all those evil things that go on in those places. You will go to work at Chicago Pneumatic and be a good toolmaker like your brother Albert."

My Father was less rigid. Several years earlier, when I was 14 years old and a freshman at Proctor, my Mother gave me a lunch to take to the Mohawk Cotton Mill where my Father worked. He slipped me in through the loading dock doors and took me on an unauthorized tour. I saw the sweat shop conditions, the backbreaking tasks, the dreary routine, the dangerous machinery. We returned to the loading dock. As we stood next to an empty freight car he said to me, "Joey, I wanted you to see how I make a living. If you don't study hard and get a good education you could end up in a place like this. I didn't have the opportunity to go to school when I was growing up, but you do." Now here he was, caught between what he had told me in private and his wife's strong stance. He would not disagree with her openly. She ran the household. He would not incur her wrath by taking an opposite position. He took a neutral path that could be interpreted by her as being supportive of her yet gave me the faint hope of his approval. When in her presence he said, "You can go do whatever you want as long as it doesn't cost any money."

Several days later I was again summoned to Mr. Huff's office. He described several scholarships that might be available to me, one of which was in Engineering with the Brown-Lipe-Chapin Division of General Motors. He explained the five year work/study program wherein I could earn each semester's tuition during alternate work periods. It sounded great. An engineer! The first college graduate in my family, and I could pay my own way. "One thing, though," he added. "You will have to pay the first semester's tuition of $600 in advance." It might as well have been a million.

That evening I excitedly told Mom and Dad about this wonderful opportunity, hoping we could find a way to raise the initial $600. Mom repeated her position, in Italian. "You are not going away from home." And Dad chimed, neutrally, "I don't care what you do as long as it doesn't cost any money."

The entrance exam was held in Syracuse. My parents reluctantly drove me there. The test took all day. That night we drove silently except for the occasional driving instructions my Mother gave my Father. Syracuse was 54 miles from Utica. This was a major trip for them and done out of love for me, despite Mom's fervent hope that I would not be chosen. Her hope was not borne out of malice, but out of love and concern for my well being and my immortal soul.

I applied for a summer job at Chicago Pneumatic as an

apprentice toolmaker. A few weeks before high school graduation I received a job offer from them.

I was also contacted by the General Motors student coordinator. He interviewed me one last time. At the end of the session he told me I had been accepted and could start the first work training session immediately after High School graduation in June. College classes would start in September. I spoke to Mom and Dad again, giving it my best sales pitch. Mom, perturbed by the news, said, "You are not going away from home. You are going to work at the Chicago Pneumatic and be a toolmaker, like your brother, Albert." And Dad repeated, neutrally, "I don't care what you do as long as it doesn't cost money."

Mr. Huff sent for me and offered congratulations. I told him I could not raise $600 for the initial semester's tuition.

During the last week of High School the wall telephone in my "home" room rang. Mrs. Nolan, my home room teacher, took the receiver off its hook, held it to her ear, listened, spoke briefly, hung up, turned and called me to her desk. "Go to the Principles office." Mr. Rollin W. Thompson usually wore a three-piece, dark suit, with pinstripes. He projected power and authority. His office was the inner sanctum where the troubled and incorrigible were made to go. I tried to imagine what I might have done to incur this sinister summons. I waited on a polished, dark walnut bench in the antechamber just outside his office while his secretary announced my presence. She came out and motioned me in. The furniture was massive, intimidating, dark and shiny. He stood, tall and immaculately dressed. He shook my hand, invited me to sit, and said, "I understand you have a scholarship from General Motors."

"Yes sir," I said.

"I also understand that you can't raise the initial tuition. Is that so?"

"Yes sir."

"If you had the tuition would you go?"

"Yes sir," I replied. I still had told no one that I also lacked permission from my parents.

"I have been talking to Mr. Huff, your teachers and the references you provided with your application." He smiled. "If you really want to go...I have a proposition for you."

I could feel my heart beating faster. Whatever he was about to say filled me with apprehension. It would cause me to make a difficult decision.

"I am prepared," he said, leaning forward in his chair, "to arrange a personal, interest free loan of $600. You can repay it after graduation. If that sounds acceptable to you I will draw up the papers and you can leave for Syracuse next week."

I was appalled. I needed time to think.

"Mr. Thompson, I really appreciate the offer. I need to talk to my parents about this. Can I let you know after we get back from our vacation? We are going to Long Branch, New Jersey, for two weeks after graduation. I can let you know when I get back." That was how we left it.

I told my parents about Mr. Thompson's offer and said I wanted to accept it. I hoped the removal of the financial burden would change their minds. I hinted that I might go without their permission. Mom was adamantly negative. "You are not going away from home to college." And Dad repeated his neutrality.

The annual family trek to Long Branch was a tradition established some four years earlier. Mom would cook, can and pack for a month ahead of time. We rented a room in the same two story, rambling hotel every year. It had a large kitchen with a dozen stoves and refrigerators so families could prepare their own meals. A large combination recreation/dining room was off the kitchen with tables, chairs, ping pong tables, a piano. The front porch ran the whole width of the hotel. The ocean, beach and salt water swimming pool were half a block away.

Over the next two weeks we had several discussions on the subject, to no avail. I thought more seriously about accepting Mr. Thompson's offer in defiance of them, but wasn't sure if I could do so. I didn't want to defy them. Still, as time passed without any change I became more desperate. I might go without permission.

We were sitting on the large front porch of the hotel one afternoon, two days before the end of our vacation. Mom had started packing that morning. She was sitting in a rocking chair, knitting. Dad sat looking into the distance at the beach that he would soon leave and would not see again for another year. I was talking to some friends of my age group when we heard a boy's voice, shouting. We looked up the street and saw him walking toward us, a stack of newspapers under one arm, waving one over his head with the other. "Extra! Extra! Read all about it! First Marine Division Ordered to Korea! Congress Orders Mandatory Draft!"

I ran down the stairs, reached into my pocket and felt for the 15 cents I had been saving all summer. I bought the paper and walked back slowly, reading the front page as my friends rubber necked over my shoulders. The article described the movement of the Marines to Korea and gave details of the proposed military draft. It said that all males of good health, 18 to 25 years old, would be drafted for service in Korea. It also said that exemptions would be granted to certain professions and full time college students enrolled in critical skills such as engineering and medicine.

I ran back to the porch and breathlessly read the article to them. My Mother looked steadily at her knitting all the time. I wondered if she had been listening. I repeated in paraphrase the parts about the draft. She said nothing. My Father looked up at me, then at her, and also said nothing.

I didn't think she understood what I had read and asked, "Mama, do you understand what this means?"

She kept knitting. "Mama?"

"Yes," she said. Then she looked up at me with damp eyes. "It means....you are going away from home to college."

I was elated. I was grateful and happy. "I'll go see Mr. Thompson and sign the loan papers........."

"No," she said softly, holding up one hand in a gesture of prevention. "We don't borrow money from strangers. This is a family affair. We will get the money. You will go with our blessings."

I floated! I soared! I was ebullient!

"Mama, I'm gonna make you proud someday! Someday, when I am rich and famous, I will buy you a mansion on a hill with a white picket fence. I will get you a private maid named Marie. And whenever you want her or need something all you'll have to do is raise your hand, crook your finger and call 'Marie!' and she will come running."

She put her knitting down and took my hand. One tear glistened on her cheek. "You have always made me proud." She gave me a shaky Mother-son kiss and picked up her knitting.

As I turned back to my friends she called after me, "Joey! When you go, you be a good boy. Remember your family. And come home once in a while!"

But I was already off the porch, running after the gang which was heading toward the beach and the sand and the surf and an unknown but exciting future.

MEMORIES OF MOM

Mom was the product of a large, loving family, early separation from her homeland, poverty ridden years in Italy followed by the great depression in the United States, a sheltered young life that did not prepare her for real life, the childhood deaths of two of her four children, all tempered by the good fortune to meet and marry a man who would love and care for her until the end.

Our home was always full of music. Both Mom and Dad drew from a broad repertoire of religious hymns, Italian ballads and operatic arias. Mom was most often humming or singing around the house, sometimes solo, sometimes accompanying radio music or our player piano. We learned early to appreciate the beauty of Italian melodies and their exquisitely emotional words. Both parents had favorite American songs, too. Mom was especially fond of "You Are Always In My Heart." It was one of the few that she knew all the words to in English. She was a hopeless romantic who saw the beauty in poetry, song and the written word. Her writings were replete with passionate turns of phrase. She believed in love and her emotions were always close to the surface.

Church was a mandatory event for Mom, three times a week for the whole family. Sunday morning was the main course followed by Tuesday evening prayer meeting. On Thursday another full service was held in hopes it would tide us over until the next Sunday. These were full bodied events lasting two hours or more. In the summer, when the weather was good for driving, we occasionally drove to Rome or Dolgeville or Frankfurt or Little Falls on Saturday or Sunday afternoon. There we attended more services at other churches of similar persuasion. I think our record was six services in one week. That is, no doubt, where I developed an intense dislike for long meetings, a feeling that carried over to adulthood.

During those long hours I learned to read Italian from the song books and bibles stuck in the little wooden pockets behind each pew. I learned how to hold my breath for over three minutes, gasping for air at the end with a stifled sound that caused the nearest sitting parishioners to look around curiously. I also learned how to hold other things for a long time because the only bathroom in the Chiesa Christiana Apostolica, the Christian Apostolic Church, was through a door up in front, on the right hand side of the altar. I had to step out of my pew into the center aisle and walk forward to the podium, turn right in front of the minister, walk across the front of the pews, open the door and enter. All eyes followed me and were waiting for me when I returned.

Central to Mom's being was the need to give to others who needed help. Over the years, as members of our church or nearby neighbors grew old and feeble, Mom adopted them and used our scant resources to bring them food and comfort.

Our close friends, the Gottusos, lived on a small farm on the outskirts of Utica. One wintery Christmas day Mom told Dad she felt the need to bring food to the Gottuso farm. A snow storm had been raging for two days. They bundled up and caught the street car that passed in front of their apartment building, each carrying two bags of groceries. At the end of the line, where Bleecker Street became a dirt road, they got off the trolley and trudged, through blowing wind, deep snow drifts and falling flakes, another mile or so. The farmhouse sat, alone, in a wide expanse of white fields. Climbing up several steps they reached the door. Dad managed to balance his bags and knock. Unbeknownst to them, Vincent and Angelina Gottuso, their grandmother and ten children had been isolated by the storm and were almost out of food.

Years later Gottuso's oldest son, Mario, recalled the scene as they opened the door and saw Mom and Dad standing there, covered in snow. "They looked like two angels, their arms bent at the elbows, holding bags of groceries. They were white with snow. It looked like they had wings. God truly answered our prayers. He sent us two angels."

Anna was a strict disciplinarian, so much so that when Albert or I did something wrong we dreaded the confrontation that would most certainly happen. Broken wooden stirring spoons and dented pasta kettles could result, even a small hole in a plaster wall from a thrown shoe. Yet, when certain severe transgressions occurred, like the time I accidentally lost our bread money, Mom would surprise us with a profound gentleness and understanding.

I recall childhood occasions when Mom spanked me for something well deserved and as I cried she would bend down to me and take my face gently in her hands and say, "Diami un bacio," ….Give me a kiss. And I would. And I knew she loved me and the punishment was just that and nothing more.

Dad worked swing-shift much of the time when Al and I were teenagers. He came home after Al and I had gone to bed. Mom reheated dinner leftovers for him. Al and I lay in bed just around the corner from the kitchen listening to the sound of silverware and plates, a spoon or fork scraping in a kettle as he ate. Mom sat at the table with him and recounted the days' adventures. Usually it was about neighbors and who had said or done what to whom. Our ears perked up when she recited some misdeed either one of us had done. We remembered her telling us to "wait 'til your Father gets home," in a threatening manner.

He listened quietly. She would feel better and by morning the issues were gone.

We had two ice boxes. One, which Dad made, was a wooden box with a lid on leather hinges. It was placed on the outdoor porch or hung from a window ledge in the winter. Milk, butter and a few other things were kept in it. In summertime we used the real ice box, located in a small closet, which had a large compartment for ice.

Mom assigned us two ice box duties. One was to take our red metal wagon three blocks to the ice house and buy ice when needed. The ice man opened a heavily insulated door in the ice house, revealing large blocks of ice packed floor to ceiling, covered with sawdust. These had been cut from one of the nearby lakes last winter and stored in the ice house. The largest block cost 50 cents. For 25 cents he cut one in half. A quarter block of ice cost 15 cents. We handed over the coins Mom had given us and hauled ice home. Dad used a pair of ice tongs to carry it upstairs then, using an ice pick, fractured and shaped the ice to fit the available space in the ice compartment.

The second job was exclusively Al's until I was old enough to take it on. That was to empty the drain pan beneath the ice box. The melting ice water collected in a pan about 18 inches across and three or four inches deep. We were expected, without being told, to check it each evening after school and empty it into the sink before it overflowed. At times we remembered it just as it started to overflow. The pan could not be moved in that condition or water would slosh all over the floor. No matter how carefully and patiently we tried to tease it forward the pan would not budge until, with a sudden lurch, it launched a Tsunami of ice water. The only safe procedure, in that case, was to lie on our stomachs, using a table spoon or tiny cup to transfer water into a smaller bowl. Since there was only a couple inches of clearance between the bottom of the ice box and the top of the pan this procedure took a good 15 to 20 minutes.

On rare occasions when we completely forgot and the pan

overflowed for several hours, water seeped through the floor and dripped through the ceiling into the shoe store below. That's when things got very ugly and Mom would utter the words that were intended to strike terror, "Wait 'til your Father comes home!"

Moms' venting to Dad was the way she released the pent up frustration of raising two boys and interacting with gossiping neighbors. Dad usually listened quietly.

One Sunday morning, I had done or said something wrong and Mom was very upset with me. We left the house to walk to church. They were walking arm in arm, as usual, and I was a few steps ahead. I could hear her recounting what I had done and what I had said which had evoked her anger. The more she spoke the more Dad fought to restrain himself. Finally, unable to contain himself any longer, he took a quick step forward and gave me a slightly more than playful kick in the rump and said something like "You shouldn't talk to your Mother that way."

Mom pulled her arm away and shouted "Vigliacco!!" at Dad. He looked stricken.

"You are mean!" she said.

"What did I do?" he asked, wide-eyed.

"You hit him!" she accused.

"Annie, what did you want me to do?" he asked with a puzzled look on his face. "You got me all worked up. What was I supposed to do?"

"Don't hit him!" she said.

And that was the way it was. Mom vented. Dad let her talk knowing he wasn't expected to do anything except listen and play the role of counselor and figurehead enforcer.

There was one notable exception to that role. I was about 15 years old when I discovered that, not only was I taller than either of my parents but, they knew nothing and I knew everything. It showed in the way I spoke to them and behaved around the house. The folks and I were in the kitchen one day when I became particularly disrespectful. Dad tried to hold his temper and talk sense to me. My retort was insolent. He took a quick step forward and, to my surprise, clutched my shirt front with one fist. The other arm hung loosely by his side. Pressing me against the wall he lifted me until my feet cleared the floor. Holding his face close to mine he said, "The only thing you've got going for you is a pretty face. If you keep talking to us like that I am going to change it." He slowly lowered me until my feet found the floor again. He released my shirt front. Mom said nothing that time. I got the point.

Mom started early on Sunday mornings to make spaghetti sauce for the afternoon meal. We got ready and left for church with the sauce in a large kettle, perking slowly over a low flame. We returned after the service several hours later. My starving senses could detect the delightful aroma of Mom's sauce as we climbed the stairs. It would be another hour before all the meats, pasta, chicken, salad and so forth was ready. Those were the longest hours I had ever experienced, before or since.

I worked evenings and weekends in the shoe store downstairs and saved my two dollars a week pay until I had twenty five dollars. Then I bought a table top radio as a birthday gift for Mom. She was so happy with the gift. A few days later she and I had an altercation, some infraction, real or imagined. Mom punished me in some form, I can't remember how, now. In my immature state of grief and pain I said something to the effect that I could have bought a lot of ice cream sodas with twenty five dollars. Mom stood stock still for a moment, then went to her bedroom and returned with twenty five dollars which she handed to me.

Shortly afterward, as Moms' sobs came from behind the closed door to her bedroom I faced my Father and told him I felt badly about what I had said and I wanted him to give her back the money.

"You were man enough to hurt her feelings, now be man enough to apologize," he advised.

It took more courage than I thought I had, but I went into

that bedroom and apologized. I asked her to please take back the money. She took my face in her hands and, through tears said, "Diami un bacio." And I did. And I knew everything was alright again.

In 1950 I went off to college. Mom wrote regularly to me, just as she had done to Albert, her letters speaking of her love and pride in us, sometimes with tear stains on them. Always she spoke of her prayers for our safety and the well being of our souls.

Every month I mailed home an aluminum case filled with soiled clothing which she returned to me laundered, ironed and folded with loving hands. During my senior year away I started to use a local laundry but Mom was upset and insisted I mail my soiled things to her. My last month at college I received the last case full of neatly cleaned and folded clothing. I still miss getting that package each month with the occasional tear stained letter inside.

I was drafted into the United States military as soon as I graduated from engineering college, at the end of the Korean War. At Mom's urging I began a correspondence with my uncle, her brother, Aneble Giangolini, who still lived in Rimini, Province of Forli, Italy. Uncle Aneble was a career military officer in the Italian cavalry where he rose to the rank of Colonnelo Maggiore or Major Colonel. He was in charge of the 300 man mounted honor guard that frequently rode in royal parades and accompanied the last King of Italy during his public appearances. With their high fur hats, sharply styled uniforms, high leather riding boots and glittering sabres they made impressive appearances in the films and photos shown in magazines and movie theatres world-wide. Mom helped me to interpret his letters and proof read my replies.

When I complained to him about military life he replied that the discipline and rigors of military life kept him young and he encouraged me to consider a military career. He did not feel age, he wrote, until he retired. Every letter ended with "un afetto abracio,"…an affectionate embrace. He owned tourist cabins on the coast of Italy in the city of Urbino and invited me to visit him. To my everlasting regret, I was unable to make the trip while he was still alive.

Rose, Nancy, Aneble and Anna Giagolini, Italy, circa 1916. This photo of Aneble was taken early in his military career. He rose to the rank of Major Colonel in the Italian Cavalry in charge of the mounted honor guard for the King of Italy, Victor Emmanuel III.

My brother Albert and his family moved to California and I followed a few years later. Mom and Dad remained in Utica. Dad became the pastor of the Christian Apostolic Church when the old pastor died. They would have liked to join us in California but remained in Utica because, they said, "As long as these people need us we must stay here." They ministered to the ageing congregation, shoveled snow off the church sidewalks in winter, made repairs to the building in summer, and took food and counsel to the ageing and increasingly dependent remaining church members. It was truly a labor of love.

In her last years Mom and Dad continued their daily walk, arm in arm, down Bleecker Street, exchanging greetings with the neighbors on those warm summer evenings in Utica. Then they would retire to their apartment and, after dinner, watch television sitting in side by side arm chairs.

During my occasional visits to Utica they tucked a small chair for me between them and Mom would hold my hand while we chatted and watched. From time to time she would rub her arthritic fingers, then admire the sparkle of her diamond ring and say, as she so often did, "When I am gone I want you to have this ring to give to the girl you marry. And tell her, this was my Mothers' ring."

Then she would take my face in her soft hands and say "Diami un bacio," and I would kiss her.

Mom and Dad were married for 54 years. At her funeral, after all others had left, only he and I stood at the casket. He lingered, then touched her one last time and I heard him say farewell to her thus, "Adio, compania mia."

"Goodbye, my companion."

I asked Dad to come back to California with me. He agreed he would do so as soon as he wrapped up his affairs and said his goodbyes. A few weeks later I flew back to Utica and brought him home.

One evening, shortly after our arrival, I took him to a small Italian restaurant in the San Fernando Valley to celebrate his birthday. They had a musical group that played both American and Italian songs. In honor of his birthday they asked if he had a favorite song. Dad requested a song called Rimpianto. They were unsure of the melody and asked him to sing a little of it. He sang it in its entirety, a capella, in Italian and in English. The formal title is Serenade by Enrico Toselli. The popular title is Rimpianto. In English it means Regret. Following are the words, loosely translated, into English:

REGRET

Like a golden dream engraved on my heart,

Remains the memory of a love, alas that lives no more.

Ah, there was her vision, smiling so sweetly,

Her shining light enthralled in joy

Our youthful days of yore.

All too brief that time for me, of such sweetly blessed joy,

It vanished, that golden dream,

And left me naught but grief.

All beyond is dark and sadder every day,

And youth itself, will soon pass away,

Lamenting, alone remains; and tears, and bitter grief of heart.

Oh, rays of sunshine,

Upon my path, alas, ye shine no more!

No more!

No more!

The restaurant erupted with applause. His eyes, and mine, were moist. They could not know, as I knew, that his song was meant for his first true love who existed, no more.

Nick and Anna circa 1956

DIALOGUES WITH DAD

About four months before his 90th Birthday, Dad was going thru what seemed like an unending series of physical setbacks that were getting him down. I asked him a hypothetical question; if dying was a simple matter of "turning the switch," without pain or suffering, would he do it? He said "Sure, if I were feeling sick and suffering." I remarked that I heard someone quoted as saying, "I am not afraid of dying, I just don't want to be there when it happens." He replied, "Everyone is afraid of dying. After all, dying is no picnic!"

For a time Dad suffered from something resembling athletes' foot, an itching and little open cracks between his toes. We tried everything, and some things seemed to help but, so far, nothing had decisively cured it. One night, after his shower, he looked at his feet, rolled his eyes heavenward, and said to heaven "Please God, another miracle to cure this affliction." I said that it would be nice if God would simply skip the sickness sometimes instead of performing miracle cures. "Wouldn't it be nice," I said "if sometimes God would say to you, 'Nick, instead of giving you measles and then curing you, I am going to skip the measles and leave you well?'"

He said, "Yes."

I said, "Well, then, you should pray, God, skip the magic show and leave my toes well." He thought a second and said, "But, you have to be sick to enjoy a miracle." And that's where we left it. The condition disappeared by itself, a few weeks later. A miracle!

I have often, over the years, used my Dad as a sounding board for my frustrations in life. Sometimes my complaints were very serious problems, often as not they were minor. Always I sought that comforting experience of having someone who loves you, unconditionally, listen and understand and be sympathetic. One day, while reciting to him several troubles in my life he placed everything in quiet perspective by observing, "Well, Joey, these are things that only afflict the living." I felt better immediately, recognizing that my problems were the normal, routine bumps in the road of life that one stops feeling only when the journey has ended.

Sometimes, when I walked into the house, Dad's TV would be blaringly loud to compensate for his diminished hearing. I would lower the volume and say something like, "Boy, that's loud, Dad!" He would reply, softly, "Joey, don't get old." At other times when I found something amiss resulting from his failing faculties I would unthinkingly admonish him. His placid reply, as always, was …"Joey, don't get old."

Now, when doctors tell me that my loss of hearing, lower back pain or absentmindedness is due to the ravages of age I tell them, truthfully, "I should have listened to my Father. He used to tell me, 'Joey, don't get old.' But I didn't listen."

My Great Aunt Mary Capalupo died October 13, 1990 at the age of 98 years and 8 months. She was Dads' Aunt, born in the same home town of Andali, Italy, nine years before him. As a young girl she babysat Dad, spending much time caring for and raising him in that rural, agricultural, starving environment of southern Italy where every girl and boy ran barefoot and no meals were guaranteed unless you were a land owner. Over the years Aunt Mary remained close to "Nicky," as she called him.

Whenever I visited her in Utica, New York, she would ask after him, speaking in the diminutive, "'Ow is Nickey? 'E is alright?" because she never stopped thinking of him as that barefoot little boy she took care of so many years ago.

A couple months before her passing I visited her for the last time. She was in excellent condition for her age, bright minded, remembering details about everyone in the family and asking perceptive questions about family members both in New York State and in California. And....she asked about "Nicky" and sent him her love. I took a video tape of her and delighted Dad with it when we returned home.

We received the phone call on a Saturday morning. We were all at home and Dad awoke bright and chipper, as usual. I waited 'til afternoon to tell him thinking it was not a good way to start off the day and not knowing how he would handle it.

"We got a phone call from Utica this morning, Dad. Aunt Mary passed away this morning. She went quietly. She didn't suffer."

I watched him carefully. He smiled softly, as if hearing that someone beloved had left on a final adventure. A kind melancholy flitted over his face and he said, "Well, that tree has seen many seasons."

He was perfectly comfortable. Dad had a strong belief system. He knew where she had gone and that he would see her again when he makes that same passage in the not-too-distant future. She will ask him about all the family members, both in New York and in California. And he will tell her.

He reminisced one day, about his childhood and what it was like when he came to the United States and he told me the following recollections:

"All I knew in English was 'son-of-a-bitch.' I learned it from a 9 year old who had visited America and returned to Italy. That and 'God Damn.' All us kids in the village learned to say 'son-of-a-bitch' and 'God Damn.'

On the farm we were paid 1 penny a day and one meal. A

good wage in Italy was 10-20 cents an hour, when you could get work. A lot of the men and boys went to America to work a while, then they went back to Italy with the money. It cost about $25-30 to cross the Atlantic, one way.

I went to school in Italy for one month only and learned the vowels; a-e-i-o-u. In Italian they are pronounced ahh, ehh ,eee, ohh, ooo. In America we settled in New Hamburg on the Hudson River, with my Father. I attended school, first grade, for one year, then we moved to Utica, New York. I went to Brandegee School, where I skipped the 2nd grade and went into the 3rd grade. I attended for one and a half years. After the first year I told the school principle, Mr. Vandenberg, 'In 6 months, when I turn 16, my Father wants me to quit school and go to work. What is the use of going to classes and studying?' He said, 'Well, OK, stay in school for the last 6 months and you can run errands for us. You won't have to attend classes.' So that was the end of my education. Mr. Vandenberg was also the President of The Savings Bank Of Utica, or, The Bank With The Gold Dome, as it was called. Later, when your Mother and I opened a savings account and went there to make deposits, he remembered me and spoke to us often.

I had a great teacher in Arithmetic, Mrs. Boardman, and one bad one, Mrs. Cook. We called her Eagle Beak because of the size of her nose. One day the boy sitting next to me reached over and put the pigtail of the girl in front of me into my inkwell. Mrs. Cook accused me of doing it. He told her he did it, but she wouldn't believe him. She picked up a switch she used to punish kids and tried to beat me with it, but I stood up and caught her arm in one hand, and took the switch from her with the other. I was small but I was tough.

If my Father had been a different type I could have done better in life. He favored Frankie, my half brother, and Bob my older brother. So I was like a "scartado." That's the leavings you get when you sort things out. Maybe he denied his fatherhood of me. Once he said to me, 'I don't know if you are my son or not.' I told him, 'I was one year old when you first left for America and 2 years old when you came back to visit. How can you doubt you are my father?'

My Mother married him when she was 16. Bob was the first born, then me. When I was one year old my Father went to America, leaving my teenage Mother alone with two children and no money.

We were hungry a lot of the time. He did not send us money. We would stand in food lines two to three hours and often they would run out before we reached the front of the line.

Once there was a terrible earthquake in Messina. It shook things so bad and did so much damage that for the next two days and nights, while the tremblers were happening, people lived in the streets, afraid to go inside the buildings. We slept in the streets for two nights, my Mother and Bob and I.

While my Father was away my Mother 'got in wrong.' He came back while she was pregnant and he beat her until she had a miscarriage. I was 2 years old when that happened.

He went back to America after that and lived with another woman and had Frankie, my half brother. When he decided that Bob and I were old enough to work he sent money for tickets for us. My Mother took us to Naples and she lived there until she could raise enough money for a one way passage for herself. Meanwhile Bob and I went on ahead to America. Later, she came to New York. The authorities called him to come and claim her. He showed up, looked at her and said, 'I don't know this woman.' They deported her back to Italy. Later, when Frankie's' mother died my father sent for my mother. She came to Utica.

He used to get drunk and when he did he beat her up. I would get between them when I was old enough to stop him, and I would say to him, 'Why didn't you leave her in Italy if you are going to treat her like this?' He claimed later that I tried to hit him with a chair. I had more respect for him than that, more than Bob or Frank. Bob drank heavily and gambled. I gave my paychecks to my father, unopened, even until two months after I was married.

My wife Annie, and I, moved downstairs with my Father after we were married. Bob, his wife and her sister moved upstairs. When my wife was 8 months pregnant my Father told her, 'Bob has two women who can do housework and cook and help me. You can't do much now. You and Nick move upstairs and let Bob and the two women move back down here with me.' One year later Bob left with his women. My Father told me to move back downstairs. I said, 'You sent my wife upstairs because she couldn't do enough work when she was pregnant. All this time she had to walk up and down those stairs with a baby. I won't make her move back down to wait on you. Now it is up to you to be a man and ask her if she wants to come downstairs to work for you.' I warned her that he might be coming to ask her. She said 'Nothing doing!' He never did ask her. He didn't have the courage.

When Bob was still living there he and I bought a piano with a roll player. After a while he stopped making his half of the payments so I bought him out. I used to play the rolls and sing. I had a strong voice. In the summertime the neighbors up and down the street used to open their windows or sit on their porches. They would yell down the street, 'Hey Nick, sing such-and-such,' and I would. They liked it and I would sing for hours.

I was lucky. I never fought in a war. I was a 15 to 16 years old during the 1st World War and in my 40s during the 2nd World War.

Well, these are some of the vignettes of my life. Some are good, some bad, some indifferent. You have to take them and like them or stay away from remembering them."

Then, he fell silent, as if he had finally unburdened himself of many heavy memories.

Left to right, Nick's father Joseph, half brother Frank, Mother Teresa Elia, and Nick. Circa 1917

ROLE REVERSAL

After Moms' death I brought Dad to Los Angeles to live with me. He was stymied by the freeway system and intimidated by the heavy traffic. He vowed never to drive again and sold his Pontiac to relatives back in Utica before the move.

He lived in my home. He had his own room which he decorated simply by hanging a couple pictures of my mother on the wall. He joined a local church and became a comfortable piece of the church circle. He went for daily walks, greeting me each night after I came home from work with stories of his daily adventures. Some days he would gather wild greens growing in a field at the top of a hill which he called Scar Face Mountain. I would come home in the evening and be greeted by the mouth watering aroma of cooking greens and beans or pasta with various vegetables. Gradually he took over much of the house gardening and when we worked out there together it was I who had to stop and rest now and then.

I was shaving in front of the bathroom mirror around 5:30 AM one Sunday. I planned to go sailing and was getting an early morning start. Dad walked into the bathroom and sat down on the commode seat cover. Dressed in his robe, he sat quietly for a few minutes and watched me shave. I became concerned because he did not usually awake this early. He was almost 79 years old. He scowled.

I said, "Are you feeling OK, Dad?"

"Ahhh! Damn women!" he replied softly.

"What?" I asked, startled.

"Women!" he repeated.

"What women, Dad? You don't have any women bothering you, do you?"

"That's just it," he answered, "You know, it's been three years since your mother died."

"Is that why you couldn't sleep," I asked? "Why don't you ask one of the women from your church to go out?"

He frowned and said "I don't know what to say, how to say it. How do you do that?"

Feeling street wise I suggested "When you are in church look around. You are bound to see two or three widows. If you see someone you like go over and say hello after the service. Ask her if she'd like to join you for a cup of coffee some time. After a while if you like her you might want to keep company with her. It's not hard, Dad."

"You really think so? Maybe I'll do that," he replied. I doubted he would but the idea seemed to cheer him up.

I went sailing and returned in the early evening. I walked through the living room to the kitchen and did a double-take as I passed his doorway. There was a woman in his room sitting next to him on the couch. I walked to the kitchen. He came out after me.

"Joey. I want you to meet somebody."

He had spotted her in church that very morning, shortly after I left to go sailing, and invited her to the house for a cup of coffee. They had been visiting with each other for several hours. I followed him to his room and was introduced to Generosa, nicknamed Genny. She was heavy set, an inch shorter than Dad, nicely dressed in a flower print dress. Her smiling round face was framed with very dark, very tight, naturally wavy hair. She greeted me brightly, like an excited child. In a slightly raspy voice with a gruff New England accent, she said she was pleased to meet me. Dad explained how they met in church that day. We visited. We talked about church and God and her family and grandkids. She told me how she left Boston some years ago after being widowed for the second time and drove across the United States with three young children. Now her children were grown and she lived with the eldest boy, Bobbie, and his family.

After a while Dad excused himself to use the bathroom. There was one within six feet, attached to his room, but he went to the far one at the other end of the house, probably for more privacy. After all, this was their first date. In his absence Genny explained, "Y'know, Nick and I are each livin' in somebody else's house. You are our kids and we love youse, but it ain't the same as being on our own. So, we been thinkin' it would be nice if we had our own place. We each get Social Security and maybe we could get our own apartment someplace. We'd get two bedrooms, y'know. We'd each have our own room." Then, after an anxious pause she added, "We wouldn't be doin' nothin' wrong."

I thought "Boy, Dad's going to be disappointed to hear that!" but I nodded and said nothing.

"Whadda ya think?" she asked. She was not afraid to ask for what she wanted. That is good, I thought, but scary. I was apprehensive. He hardly knew her. I answered with a non-committal, "Whatever makes my father happy will make me happy, Genny."

Dad returned and Genny took her cue to go to the far bathroom. "Well, what do you think of her? Does she seem OK to you?" he asked. I said I hardly knew her. He replied, "Yes, but you know more about women than I do. I want to know what you think." I allowed that she seemed nice.

"Did she tell you what we were thinking?" he asked.

His need for my approval surprised me and I felt the burden of parenthood descending on my shoulders. "Well, as I said, she seems nice," I answered, "but maybe you should get to know her and her family a little better before you make that commitment."

He smiled. I drove her home to Bobbie's house out in Orange County, traveling 50 miles through heavy traffic on the Interstate 5 Freeway.

She and Dad spoke on the phone several times every day, for hours. Increasingly I had to ask him to get off the phone so I could use it. They were like teenagers. If he wasn't calling her, she was calling him. They came over after church each Sunday and spent the day together. Several times I drove him out to her house for the day and Bobbie would return him in the evening.

One morning he came to me and asked if he could borrow the car. "Really?" I asked. "What for?"

"I want to go out to Genny's house. I'll be back tonight."

I was terrified. I feared for his safety. I worried he would be rattled by the Los Angeles freeway traffic or get lost. I swallowed hard, then handed him the keys. I followed him around the house as he spiffed himself up and prepared to go. I walked him out to the car. I urged him to drive carefully, to call if he needed help and not be too late getting back. As he started the engine and lowered the window to say goodbye I could not resist saying, "Call me when you get there."

This was the first time he had driven a car in over three years and the very first time in Los Angeles. He drove slowly away. I stood in the street watching the car reach the far corner and turn downhill toward the city. I stood there for several moments after it was out of sight. That night I lay awake until I heard the car pull into the driveway and the house door open and close. Dad had become the child and I, the parent. I bought another car and gave him mine.

They did not move in together. Instead, Dad made that trip many times over the next year until they were married. We had a small wedding ceremony in the church where they met. My wedding present was a week at an ocean side hotel in Redondo

Beach with a third floor balcony overlooking the romantic harbor. We told no one where they were going so they would not be disturbed.

Early the next morning Dad called me at work and asked if I would stop by that evening with a couple bottles of champagne from the gifts they had received. After work I drove home, picked up two bottles, and drove to the hotel. I called their room from the desk and told Dad I would leave the champagne at the desk.

"No, no," he said. "Bring it up. We want to see you."

So, I took the elevator up carrying a champagne bottle in each hand. The door was ajar. Dad threw it open. Two champagne bottles lay empty on the dresser. Dad was in his under shorts. Genny was wearing her nightgown. The balcony door was slid open, a warm ocean breeze swaying the filmy curtains. The bed was unmade. They were smiling broadly. Both looked sheepish, impish and giddy.

Dad grinned and said, "We drove to the house this morning and got a couple bottles already."

"Wow," I said. "It looks like you two have been having a party all day!"

Genny rasped happily, "We checked everyt'ing out an' everyt'ing still works!"

They insisted that I stay and have a drink with them.

We opened another bottle and drank a toast to each other and to "...t'ings that still work!"

EPILOGUE

Nick and Generosa were married for ten years. In 1989 Genny passed away. Nick remained a widower until his death in 1993 at the age of 93.

Big brother Albert passed away in 2004 at the age of 81, dying peacefully in his sleep.

When Anna—Mom—died at the age of 72, in 1976, Albert and I were living in California and had no forewarning that she was ill. We flew out the next day. Visitation was over within 24 hours. The funeral service followed immediately and was short. There was no graveside service as it was winter and the ground was frozen and covered with snow. A visiting pastor gave a short sermon complete with prayers and the standard funereal songs including "God Be With You 'Til We Meet Again." The format was in the old style in which no one was invited to speak or give a eulogy. Further, it would not have been comfortable to do so in English as most would not have understood. Attendees were largely elderly Italian church members who spoke little English. As a consequence there was no opportunity to give a tribute to Mom. It is my hope that, through the writings in foregoing chapters, the reader can glean the love, beauty and passion that was Anna, beloved wife and Mother. If so, Anna's eulogy has now been delivered.

I did have the opportunity to present eulogies for Nick—my Father—and Albert—my brother. They follow.

TRIBUTE TO NICHOLAS G. MANFREDO

Delivered at Calvary Assembly of God Church December 13, 1993

Nicholas G. Manfredo was my Father and my friend. He was born on August 19, 1900, at the beginning of a new century, in the small village of Andali, Province of Catanzaro, State of Calabria, located in the heel of Italy. Dad said if you stood on the hilltop of the cemetery behind the village church you could see all the way to the Ionion Sea.

He was raised in poverty. At an early age he began working at his Uncle's farms. At the age of 12 he immigrated to the United States. His life was spent as a general laborer, working with his muscles, depending on physical strength. He had little schooling, but he carried the wisdom of the ages.

He met and married Anna Giangolini who remained his wife for 54 years. During the early years of his marriage to Anna they converted to the Pentecostal faith. He eventually became the

Pastor of the Christian Apostolic Church in Utica, New York and ministered to that congregation until 1976 when Anna passed away. Nick then moved to Los Angeles to be with his children. Here he met and married Generosa Fuoco, his wife for ten years. They were members of the Calvary Assembly of God church.

Nick lived just over 93 years. He left this life willingly and enthusiastically with the sure knowledge that he was going to be with his beloved Lord. He is survived by five sons, Joseph Manfredo of Palos Verdes, Albert Manfredo of Nevada, Frank Fuoco of Lomita, David Fuoco of Carson, and Robert Iannessa of Lakewood; a daughter, Diane Patuto of Massachusetts, a brother, Frank of New York, 19 grandchildren, seven great-grandchildren; and one great-great-grandchild.

I remember how, when I was a child, he carried me up and down the three long flights of stairs of our home effortlessly, as if I weighed nothing. I thought he was the strongest man on earth. Only later did I learn of his massive inner strength that lay in his Faith in God, his integrity and his love for his fellow man. I wanted to be like him when I grew up, but I have never been able to match his power of conviction.

During his many years of service to God he demonstrated a love and charity which only those who received it can fully describe. In his youth he often brought food and the Word of God to the needy. Later, when he had less worldly things to share, he continued to dispense spiritual food. He had the kind word, the cheerful, encouraging phrase, the message that said he believed in you and everything would come together for good to them that love God. He ministered to people all his life, to the very end.

As he grew older he would sometimes wonder why God had called so many of his friends and relatives home but left him here on Earth. But there was always someone who needed him and he would say, "That is why God has left me here. I still have His work to do."

Nick had a powerful and beautiful singing voice. He especially loved the old religious hymns. With no formal musical training he taught himself to sight read music and would introduce new hymns to the church. His testimony was always accompanied by his music.

People always spoke highly of Dad, but they began to come forward more so as his health failed. The people from the Salvation Army "Meals On Wheels" told me he was their favorite stop. He invited them in and spoke of God and love and sometimes sang for them. They said, "We call him 'Mr. God Bless You.' "

The patients and staff at the convalescent home, where he spent his last days, came to me, one at a time, to express their sorrow and love. "He was an inspiration," they said.

A few days ago he was feeling unusually spry and he began to sing hymns. They placed him in a wheel chair and moved him throughout the home, singing special requests from his hymn book. That night when I visited him he was glowing with joy. "This is why God is keeping me here," he said, "to bring the Lord's music to these people."

The next day he felt tired. "Too much singing," he thought, "too many encores." He began to fail rapidly. One little nurse came in and held his hand. She had been especially attentive to him over the last weeks and I thanked her for what she had done for him. "Oh No," she said, "I am grateful for what he has done for me! He has blessed me with words and music. I didn't understand some of the language, but it was all so beautiful. He made me feel so good."

In one of our last conversations he said to me, "I am sorry that you have to see me this way. But I am tired now. My work is finished here. I want to go home."

So Nick went home. He is at peace. This is the day he waited 93 years for.

I feel sorrow for myself and for those of you who share this loss. We will miss him.

But I am happy for him,..........for now he is singing with the angels.

Nicholas Manfredo, circa 1920.

Tribute to Albert

Delivered at the 2005 Gotttuso Family Reunion

Albert Manfredo was born on March 9, 1923 in Utica, New York, USA. He was my big brother.

Al was a quiet man, not given to bragging, not volunteering to be noticed, so there may be a few things about him that you don't know. I would like to tell you a little about him. Many of the people who knew Al and loved him are here today, so this seems like a good idea.

Al and I were born 9 years apart. Our age difference meant that he was sometimes unfairly held responsible for any problems that came up between us. After all, I was the little brother and he was the big brother.

Albert and I spent a lot of time together because Mom made him take me with him wherever he went. One of the things we often did together was to take the street car from Bleecker and Mohawk Street, East on Bleecker Street all the way to the end of the line. From there we walked along dirt roads past an old boxing ring, past some old wooden buildings where they made fireworks and finally to a small farm where the Gottuso's lived. We spent many happy days there. We didn't know, then, that relationship would continue all our lives.

Al took piano lessons as a kid. He played the organ at church services in the Christian Apostolic Church in Utica. Each year the congregation got older. And each year they sang more slowly. Over the years Al struggled to get them to keep up with the music. No matter how hard he pumped the old foot pedals, no matter how loud he played the notes, the old folks lagged just a couple more notes behind the music with each passing year.

Al graduated from Proctor High School in Utica with honors. He was inducted into the National Honor Society in his Junior Year. He went to work at The Savage Arms Corporation as an apprentice toolmaker.

In the early 1940's Al was drafted into the United States Army and served in the Second World War. He was sent to the Pacific Theatre. On the day they shipped out of San Francisco his buddies were issued the standard M1A1 Garand Rifle. Al was issued a pistol and a combat knife. This puzzled Al. He reminded them that he was a conscientious objector and could not kill anyone. They said that was perfect. They intended to smuggle him behind enemy lines, with a radio, to observe and report enemy positions and strength. They said, "We don't want you to kill anyone...that would give away your position. If you get caught by the Japanese maybe you'll think of a use for these weapons." So there was Christian Soldier Albert, marching off to war with a radio.

But God had other plans for Albert. Enroute to the invasion of Okinawa a Pacific typhoon forced his convoy to take a detour of a thousand miles or so. By the time Al's ship reached Okinawa the invasion was two days old and combat lines were several miles inland. Al's unit never quite made it to the front.

Albert was among the first troops to land in Japan after the surrender and he was in the first truck convoy to enter Hiroshima and Nagasaki, the cities that had been leveled by atomic bombs.

He told me many stories. Let me tell you just one. Al was the Supply Sergeant in Nagasaki. It was winter in Japan. He took a truck and a few of his men to a warehouse at the edge of town to bring back some pot bellied stoves. At the warehouse he reached out to pick up a stove....it crumbled into gray dust. The heat of the atomic blast had reduced the heavy cast iron to ash so instantly that they remained upright and appeared in perfect condition until they were touched. Al marveled that something could look so normal, so perfect, but have no real substance. He considered it a metaphor of life.

After the war Al returned to Utica. He worked all week and commuted by bus to Rome every weekend to court Rose Gottuso. Of course, I went with him.

After the birth of their first child, Annette, they followed the Gottusos to California. Here their son, Nicholas, was born. Many years later, after Al's marriage to Beverly, he adopted another daughter, Charlene. At last count he had five grandchildren and seven great-grandchildren.

Al became an instrument maker, the highest level of expertise that a machinist can reach. During the Cold War years he worked on "top secret" projects at Jet Propulsion Laboratories. He was guarded by an armed soldier while he worked. Whenever a particularly difficult challenge arose they would come to Al, their most senior instrument maker, and ask him to devise a way to get it done. And he would.

In later years Al was one of only two instrument makers who could do the precise work necessary to manufacture the Panavision camera. If you have seen a movie in the last few decades it was probably shot with one of Al's cameras.

Some years ago my life took a very rough turn, one that really had me on the ropes. Al knew something was wrong and he came to talk to me. He asked me what was going on.....and I told him.

Then he gave me a little grin, and a hug,
and he said to me......"I'm with you, little brother."

And I felt comforted and I didn't feel alone anymore.

When he passed on, June 26, 2004, at the age of 81 years and 3 months, he did it the way he lived, quietly, peacefully. He left us in his sleep.

Afterward Beverly, his second wife, gave me the Grandfather clock that Al loved to listen to. He said it comforted him during the long nights of his last years.

Now, when I hear the clock chime, I like to think he is speaking to me......

The way he used to,

Whispering to me,

When I need to hear it....

"I'm still with you, little brother.......I'm still with you."

Albert Manfredo, 1923–2004

APPENDIX

MANFREDO FAMILY HISTORY

The Manfredi's were one of the five ruling families whose city-state kingdoms comprised the lands which would later become known as Italy. The Vatican was one of the ruling entities back then. Under Pope Borgia several of the other ruling family kingdoms were conquered. Borgia's forces managed to kill Manfredi senior who was then succeeded by his young teenage son. Pope Borgia then sent peace emissaries to invite young Manfredi to Rome to make peace. He went. He was assassinated after being abused and tortured. Years later a military invasion led by Giuseppe Garibaldi drove out the foreign occupiers and eventually resulted in a united Italy. Some remnants of the Manfredi family dynasty probably remain, to this day, ensconced along the eastern coast or in the southern part of Italy in the State of Calabria.

There is a boulevard in Florence, Italy named Viale Manfredo Fanti. It is horseshoe shaped and surrounds a very large sports complex that houses, among other venues, soccer stadiums and a baseball diamond. Further north, up the eastern coast is a gulf named Golfo de Manfredi.

MANFREDO FAMILY CREST

The following information is contained on an 11 inch by 14 inch paper procured by my brother Albert from an organization called "The Historical Research Center." Its authenticity remains for others to determine.

****

FAMILY NAME HISTORY: It is indeed not surprising that one of the first Western European countries, after the fall of the Roman Empire, to institute hereditary surnames was Italy. There is documentary evidence to show that hereditary names were employed among the patricians of the Republic of Venice in the tenth and eleventh centuries. As among the Romans, where a gens-name, derived from the founder of the family tree, was added in the praenomen, or first name, so too among the Venetians the "cognomen," a "family name," was derived from a name applied to an earlier ancestor. This name was itself derived from a number of very diverse sources.

The Italian surname Manfreddi (and its variants Manfredi, Manfredo, Manfrida and Manfredini is of patronymic origin, that is, derived from the first name of the father of the initial bearer. In this instance, the name indicates "son of Manfreddi," an Italian form of Manfred. The personal name Manfred is of Germanic origin, derived from the Old High German "man," meaning "man" and fridu", meaning "peace." This name was Latinized as Manfredus, Manfridus and Maginfredus and documented in Lomabardy as early as the eight century.

Early records show that one Manfredi from Faenza resided in Padua in 1081 where the family were members of the nobility and the governing counsel. Fiorente Manfredi resided in Cremona in 1112 and Manfredo Manfredi was a doctor of Law and ambassador in Trevigioni in 1318. In 1334 one Riccardo Manfredi was living in Avignon. The blazon of arms described below is associated with the name or a variant.

BLAZON OF ARMS: Azure, on a terrace argent, a tree vert. In front of the tree a lion passant of the second and in chief two Fleur-de-lis

TRANSLATION: The tree indicates Antiquity and Strength and the lion indicates Courage, Strength and Generosity. The Fleur-de-Lis denotes Faith, Wisdom and Valour.

CREST: The fleur-de-lis of the arms.

ORIGIN: Italy

GIANGOLINI FAMILY SHIELD

My copy of the Giangolini heraldic family shield is very old and is mounted on a 7 ½ by 10 inch cardboard backing with hand coloring of the shield. The crown and left hand side, which contains an eagle, is silver. The right hand side has a blue cross on a crimson background. It was given to me by my Mother, Anna Giangolini Manfredo. This is a numbered copy. On the original, just to the right of the shield you can faintly make out the certification ink stamp. Two words are illegible and the number is faded but the word ROMA (Rome) is still visible. At the lower right hand side is a notation that this information comes from the Heraldic Journal, Volume 1, from the Vittorio Emanuele Biblioteca which I assume is in Rome.

I used a computer translation program first, then looked up some of the words the computer had trouble deciphering. Words I looked up in the Italian/English and then Webster's English dictionaries were:

Gonfaloniere
gonfalon
rimonta
Patrio Statuto
Esimio preside

Using this information and what little knowledge I have of the Italian states during Medieval Italy, and remembering what my Mother told me, I have pieced together the following translation:

The original family was from Florence. Its origin arose around 1250 in the person of one ANTONIO of GIANGOLINI, a valiant solder. His descendants were called GIANGOLINI. TITO was one of the Reformers of the Fatherland's Constitution in 1462. A branch bloomed (flourished) in Bologna since about 1690 and another in the Marches. CIRIACO was a distinguished principle of Florence in 1699. The GIANGOLINI, for approximately two centuries, had enjoyed Noble status in the State of Florence. MARCO was a Prince of the State of Florence.

CHRONOLOGY

1900 Dad (Nicholas Gioachino Manfredo) was born in Andali, province of Catanzaro, State of Calabria, Italy in August.

1903 Mom (Anna Giangolini) was born in Vignanello, Italy, just 15 miles from Rome.

1912 Dad immigrated to America.

1920 Mom immigrated to America

1922 Mom and Dad married April 22, at St. Mary of Mt. Carmel church in Utica, New York. Dad was 21, Mom was 18 years old.

1923 Albert was born.

1925 Augustine was born. He lived for thirteen months and died from childhood disease.

1927 Nicholas Jr. was born. Died in infancy.

1932 Joseph was born Sept 14th. Dad was 32, Mom was 29, and Albert was 9 yrs old.

1976 Mom died in 1976 at the age of 73

1979 Dad married Generosa Fuoco

1989 Generosa died

1993 Dad died just before his 94th birthday.

2004 Albert died. He was 81 years old.

GEOGRAPHIC NOTES

ANDALI, ITALY

Google information, as of July 2008, describes Andali, Italy as located at Latitude 39 degrees, 1 minute, 0 seconds North, Longitude 16 degrees, 46 minutes, 0 seconds East.

Andali is located in the foothills of a mountain range, just inland and north from coastal lowlands which stretch to the beaches of the Ionian Sea. Its climate has been compared to that of Southern California which sits roughly at Latitude 33 degrees, 49 minutes north. Although 6 degrees further north, southern Italy's climate is tempered by being surrounded on three sides by seas.

Population is 954 of which 470 are male, 484 are female. It is 53.2 square miles with 371 families and 622 housing units. Andali has 33 churches, one for every 28.9 people.

Circling the outskirts of the town is a highway, SP 259, also known as the John F. Kennedy autostrada.

VIGNANELLO, ITALY

Google information, as of June, 2009 describes Vignanello, Italy as located in central Italy, north of Rome in the Lazio Region, Province of Viterbo. Vignanello has a population of 4,705 comprised of 1,800 families living in 2,402 housing units.

GIUSEPPE GARIBALDI

Giuseppe Garibaldi attained international fame as the man who was responsible for the eventual unification of Italy into one nation. He waged a number of military campaigns and by 1860 he had succeeded in unifying much, but not all, of the country. Rome and its many possessions, ruled by the Holy See, remained independent from Italy under protection from French troops. The rightful Pope, Pius IX, who favored a united Italy, remained in exile while the Holy See, in the Vatican, supported by French troops, fought unification.

As an interim move Garibaldi delivered the liberated territories of Italy to the autocratic rule of King Victor Emmanuel.

An interesting, but little known fact, is that in 1861 Garibaldi volunteered his service to Abraham Lincoln during the American Civil War on one condition—that Lincoln proclaim the war's objective to be the abolishment of slavery. Lincoln offered him command of the northern forces in 1862 but was not prepared to state abolition as the war's objective for fear it would disrupt the agricultural economy of the nation. Garibaldi declined the offer. He continued his campaigns to free the rest of Italy from the Holy See in Rome in the hope that as one nation Italy would eventually become a Republic.

In 1862 Garibaldi invaded the Italian mainland through Melito in the State of Calabria and drove north in an attempt to take Rome and its territories from the Holy See. When that campaign failed due to the French armies he joined French revolutionaries who sought to overthrow the French royal family. They succeeded and France became a Republic. The French armies were withdrawn from Rome finally returning the city and all its territories to one united Italy in 1870. Italy remained a kingdom for another 76 years.

Garibaldi died in 1882 at the age of 75.

After World War II his dream finally became a reality. In 1946 Italy officially became a Republic, similar to France and the United States.